PUSH
STITCHERY

PUSH
STITCHERY

30 Artists Explore the Boundaries of Stitched Art

Curated by Jamie Chalmers

LARK
Asheville

LARK CRAFTS

An Imprint of Sterling Publishing
387 Park Avenue South
New York, NY 10016

Text © 2011, Lark Crafts, an Imprint of Sterling Publishing Co., Inc.
Photography © 2011, Artist/Photographer

All rights reserved. No part of this publication may be reproduced, stored in a retrieval system, or transmitted, in any form or by any means, electronic, mechanical, photocopying, recording, or otherwise, without prior written permission from the publisher.

ISBN 978-1-60059-787-9

Library of Congress Cataloging-in-Publication Data

Push stitchery : 30 artists explore the boundaries of stitched art.
   p. cm.
  Includes index.
  ISBN 978-1-60059-787-9
  1. Fiberwork--History--21st century. 2. Stitches (Sewing) I. Lark Crafts (Firm)
  N6498.F54P87 2011
  746.09'051--dc22
                     2010053439

Distributed in Canada by Sterling Publishing
c/o Canadian Manda Group, 165 Dufferin Street
Toronto, Ontario, Canada M6K 3H6
Distributed in the United Kingdom by GMC Distribution Services
Castle Place, 166 High Street, Lewes, East Sussex, England BN7 1XU
Distributed in Australia by Capricorn Link (Australia) Pty. Ltd.
P.O. Box 704, Windsor, NSW 2756, Australia

For information about custom editions, special sales, and premium and corporate purchases, please contact Sterling Special Sales at 800-805-5489 or specialsales@sterlingpublishing.com.

Email academic@larkbooks.com for information about desk and examination copies. The complete policy can be found at larkcrafts.com.

The works represented in this book are the original creations of the contributing artists. All artists retain copyright on their individual works.

The photographs and text in this volume are intended for the personal use of the reader and may be reproduced for that purpose only. Any other use, especially commercial use, is forbidden under law without written permission of the copyright holder.

Manufactured in China

2 4 6 8 10 9 7 5 3

larkcrafts.com

EVEN EEN
DROPJE
any reply
may be
read by me
or others
DO NOT CROSS
DEADLOCK
WETLOOK
AFTER
WE SAW
THEM
..FRIENDLY..?
FIRE...
DOUBLE YOUR FULL
UK BREAKFAST
FOR JUST 2£ MORE
PEOPLE WITH
PACEMAKERS
STRONG
MAGNETS
ELECT
-RO
the PURCHA
-SE
OF A
CAR
in 1917
PRE RINSE
EVEN
CLEAN HA
NDS CAN
DAMAGE!
Flippin'
AWESOME!!
WE DID THE LOO FIRST
AT THE
PEEP
yes
OR RUN AS THIS TENDS TO CAUSE PANIC

CONTENTS

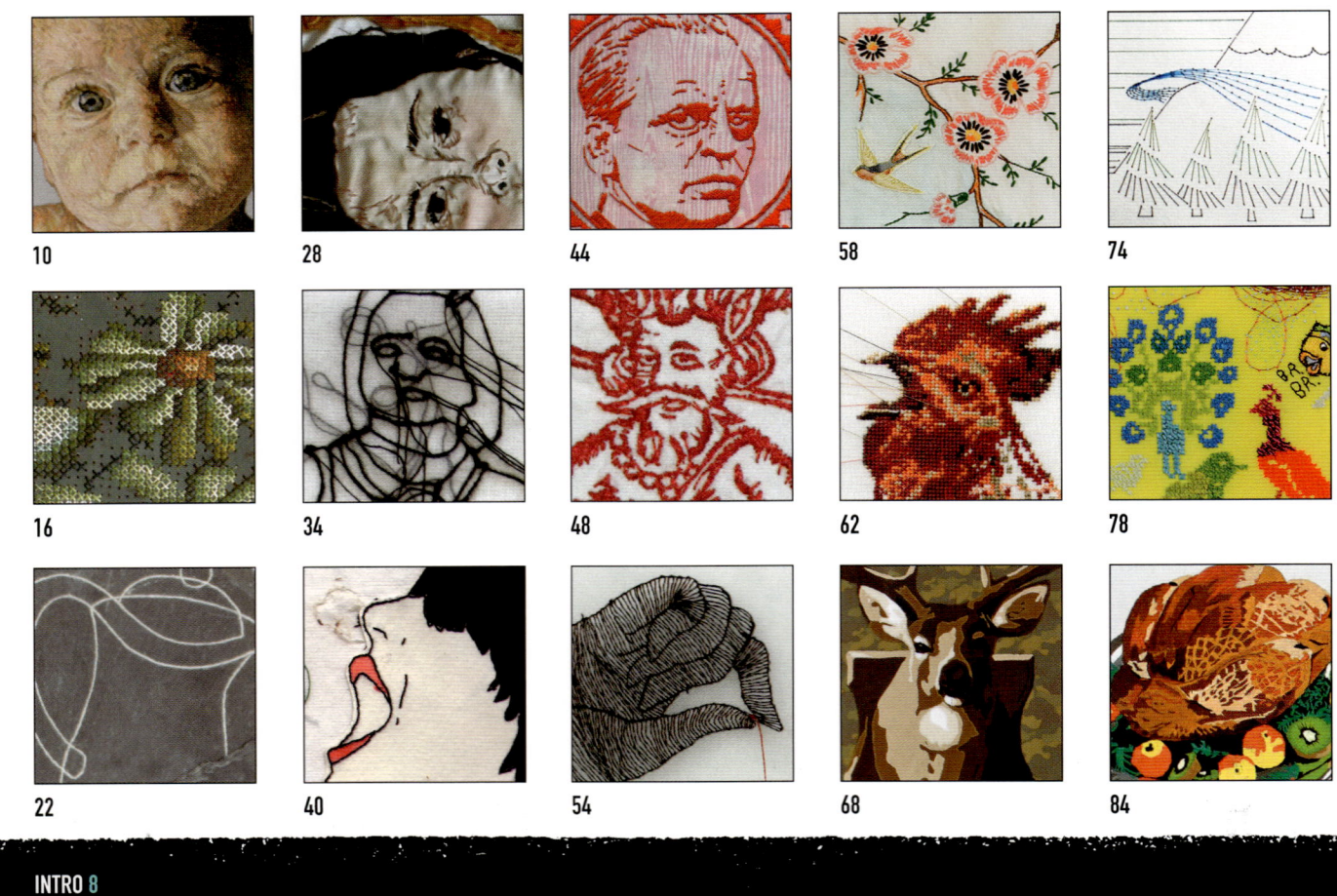

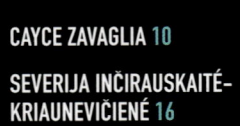

INTRO 8

CAYCE ZAVAGLIA 10

SEVERIJA INČIRAUSKAITÉ-KRIAUNEVIČIENÉ 16

CLYDE OLLIVER 22

JOETTA MAUE 28

ROSIE JAMES 34

RAQUEL J. ALVES 40

PENNY NICKELS 44

BASCOM HOGUE 48

DIEM CHAU 54

ORLY COGAN 58

ALICIA ROSS 62

LUKE HAYNES 68

PETER CRAWLEY 74

TILLEKE SCHWARZ 78

JENNIFER BOE 84

90

108

124

136

150

96

114

128

142

156

102

118

132

146

162

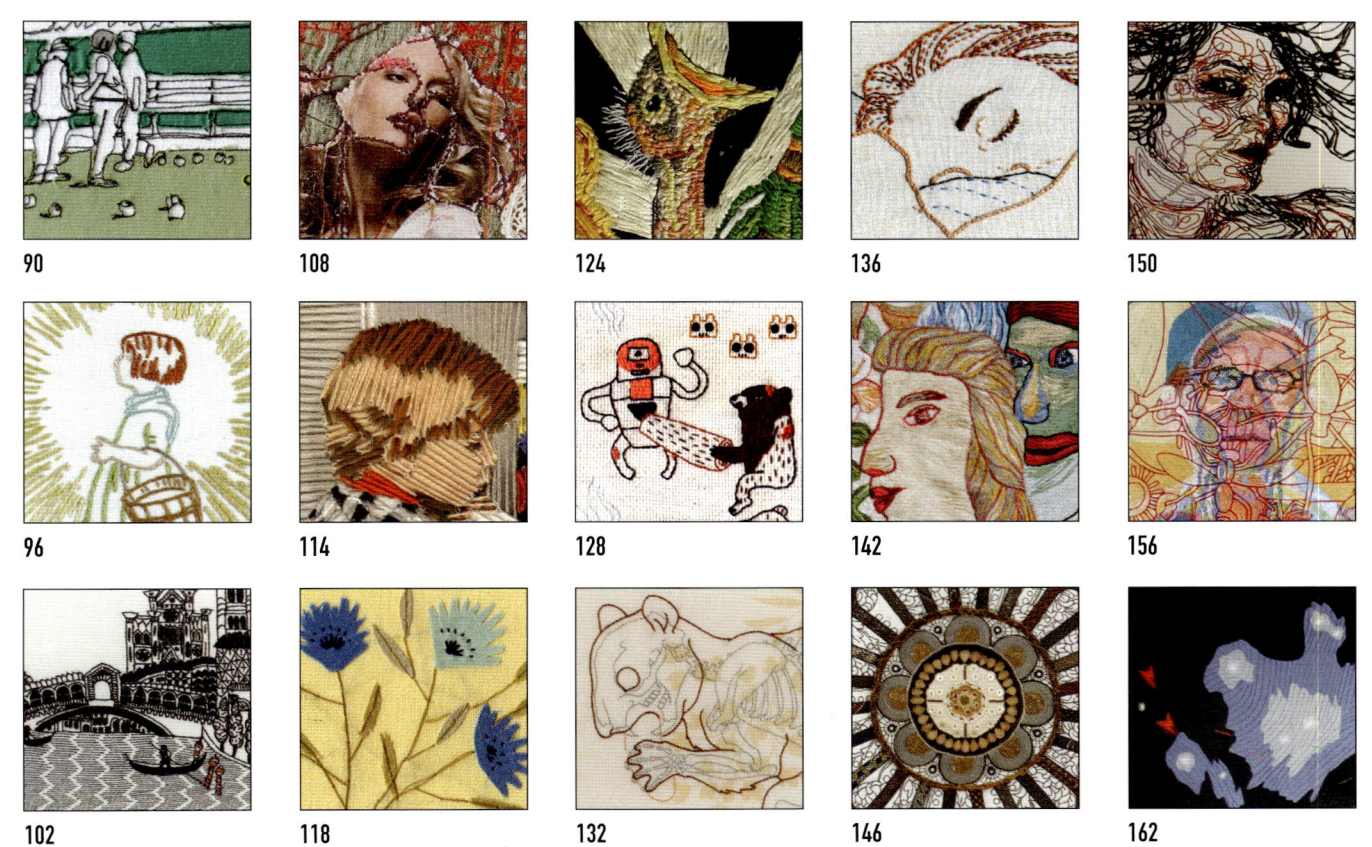

GILLIAN BATES 90

JENNIFER L. PORTER 96

CHARLENE MULLEN 102

MARLOES DUYKER 108

CÉCILE JARSAILLON 114

EMILY EIBEL 118

WILLIAM SCHAFF 124

AYA KAKEDA 128

ANDREA VANDER KOOIJ 132

MEAGAN ILEANA 136

ANNA TORMA 142

DONNA SHARRETT 146

LOUISE RILEY 150

ROBERT FORMAN 156

JIMMY MCBRIDE 162

THE ARTISTS/INDEX 168

ACKNOWLEDGMENTS/
ABOUT THE JUROR 175

INTRO

Welcome to *PUSH*, an exciting gallery series exploring contemporary artists who "push" the boundaries of traditional craft mediums. Here in *PUSH Stitchery*, you'll be blown away by what can be accomplished with a simple needle and thread, as artists reshape our understanding of embroidery, needlecraft, quilting, and textile arts. These pages contain the beautiful and provocative works of 30 talented stitchers from across the globe.

It has been such a pleasure to curate this book—as a stitcher, myself, I have been hugely inspired by the artworks you are about to enjoy. My story began with cross-stitch, which I still refer to as a "gateway" craft. Shortly after that, I began blogging about stitching, soon discovering other people who were producing contemporary cross-stitch, snarky samplers, and genre-busting free-style pieces. It was a revelation.

Across the world individuals are exploring the scope of what can be done when tradition meets innovation. Many of the artists I selected for this publication are working in relative isolation, unable to share their art within their own communities; yet on the Internet, they have found ways to interact with one another. Craft websites and image hosting sites provide a mechanism for people to show their works and share their diverse cultural references. I found an amazing community of like-minded stitchers there, and I never looked back.

From needlepoint and cross-stitch to quilting and appliqué, artists today are re-appropriating traditional techniques and making new statements with them. Conventional styles are being combined with new influences to create subversive pieces; stitching becomes a tool for exploring angst, rage, sexuality, and for examining social phenomena. And it remains a vehicle for creating pieces of art that are powerful and breathtaking.

Although fabric remains the material of choice for the majority, unorthodox surfaces like metal and stone make an appearance in some of the most fascinating works you'll see here. Each time someone pushes the boundaries, it opens creative space for other people to explore, and the movement continues. In an increasingly electronic age, stitchery provides a tangible documentation of contemporary culture, and the creations of today are our future heirlooms and artefacts.

Jamie "Mr. X Stitch" Chalmers

INTRO

JAMIE CHALMERS · UNITED KINGDOM ·

photo by: **LOUISE POLLARD**

CAYCE ZAVAGLIA
UNITED STATES

"Although my medium is crewel embroidery with wool, the technique borrows more from the worlds of drawing and painting."

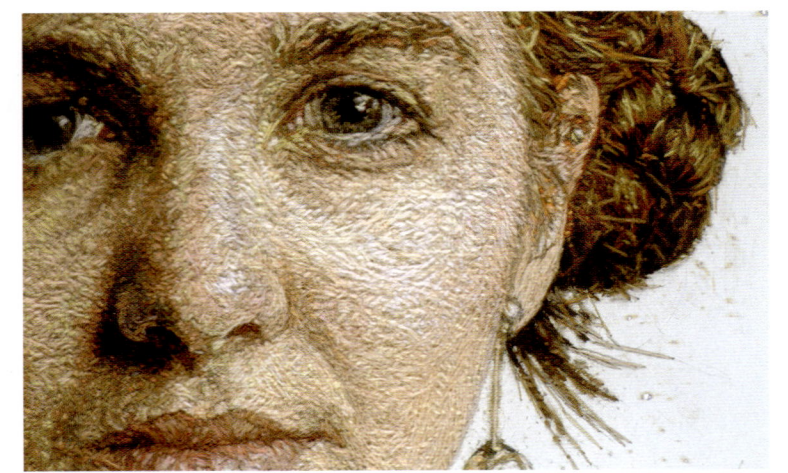

SOPHIE
2007 | 14 × 35 inches (35.6 × 88.9 cm)
Crewel wool and acrylic on linen; hand embroidered
Photos by artist

DAD
2007 | 14 x 39 inches (35.6 x 99.1 cm)
Crewel wool and acrylic on linen;
hand embroidered
Photo by artist

Q&A

HOW DO YOU DESCRIBE YOUR WORK? I still consider myself a painter, and I find it difficult not to refer to these embroidered portraits as "paintings." The direction in which the threads are sewn mimics the way lines are layered in a drawing to give the illusion of depth, volume, and form. My work unabashedly nods its head to the tradition of tapestry and my own love of craft. Using wool instead of oils has allowed me to broaden the dialogue between portrait and process as well as propose a new definition for the word "painting." **HAS YOUR WORKING PROCESS EVOLVED OVER TIME?** I am continually learning about the possibilities of working with wool—the way it can be manipulated, the way it can be

CAYCE ZAVAGLIA

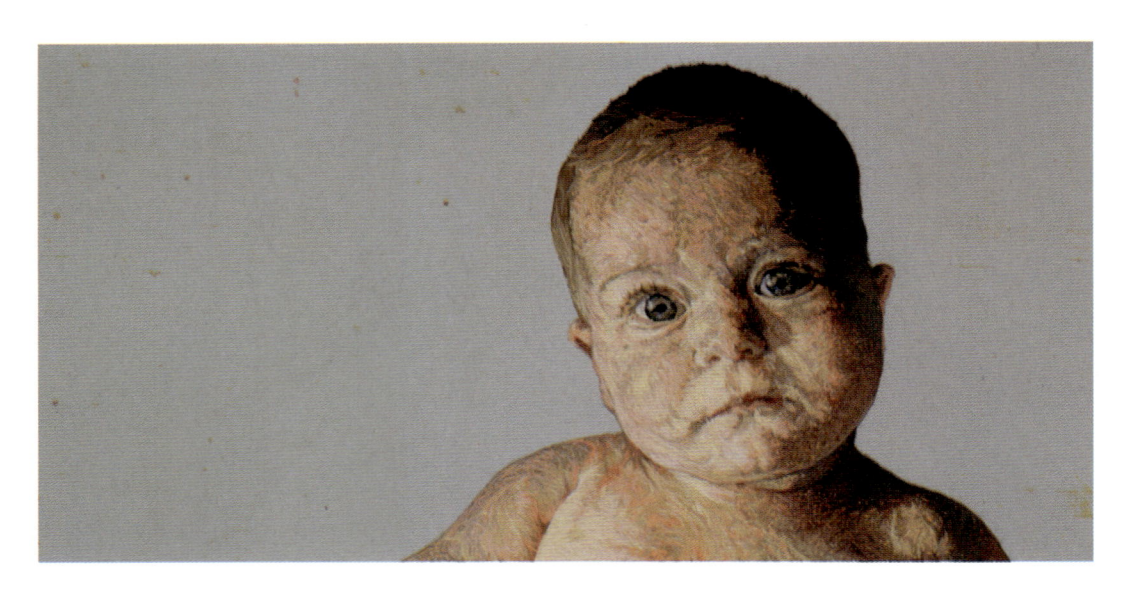

RAPHAELLA
2002 | 10 x 18 inches (25.4 x 45.7 cm)
Crewel wool and acrylic on linen;
hand embroidered
Photo by artist

AUNT LIN
2009 | 16¼ x 29 inches (41.3 x 73.7 cm)
Crewel wool and acrylic cn linen;
hand embroidered
Photo by artist

layered and combined with other colors, the way it can be sanded down to then sew a thin, fine line. Over time my stitches have become tighter and more complex but ultimately more evocative of flesh, hair, and cloth. My first piece was very loose in construction and was made using only about 30 colors of wool. My most recent piece features multi-layered stitching, is much more obsessive, and was made using over 200 colors of wool. The technique has developed as I have worked from portrait to portrait and experimented with the material. **TELL US ABOUT YOUR SUBJECT MATTER.** My subject matter has remained constant over the last fifteen years and continues to focus primarily on the portraits of family, friends, and fellow artists. I have yet to become bored with documenting those dearest to me.

14

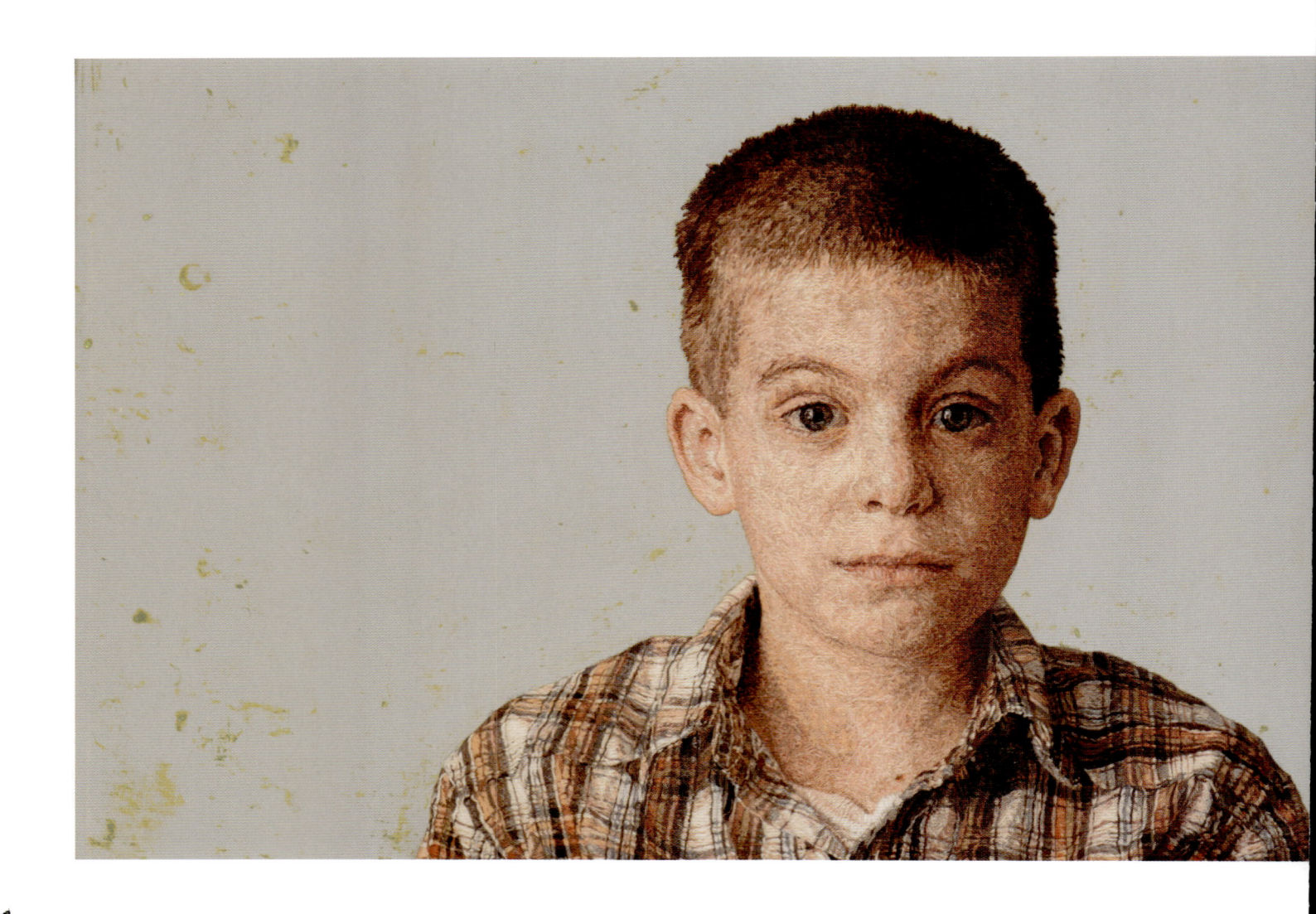

◀ **TEO**
2010 | 12 x 34 inches (30.5 x 86.4 cm)
Crewel wool and acrylic on linen;
hand embroidered
Photos by artist

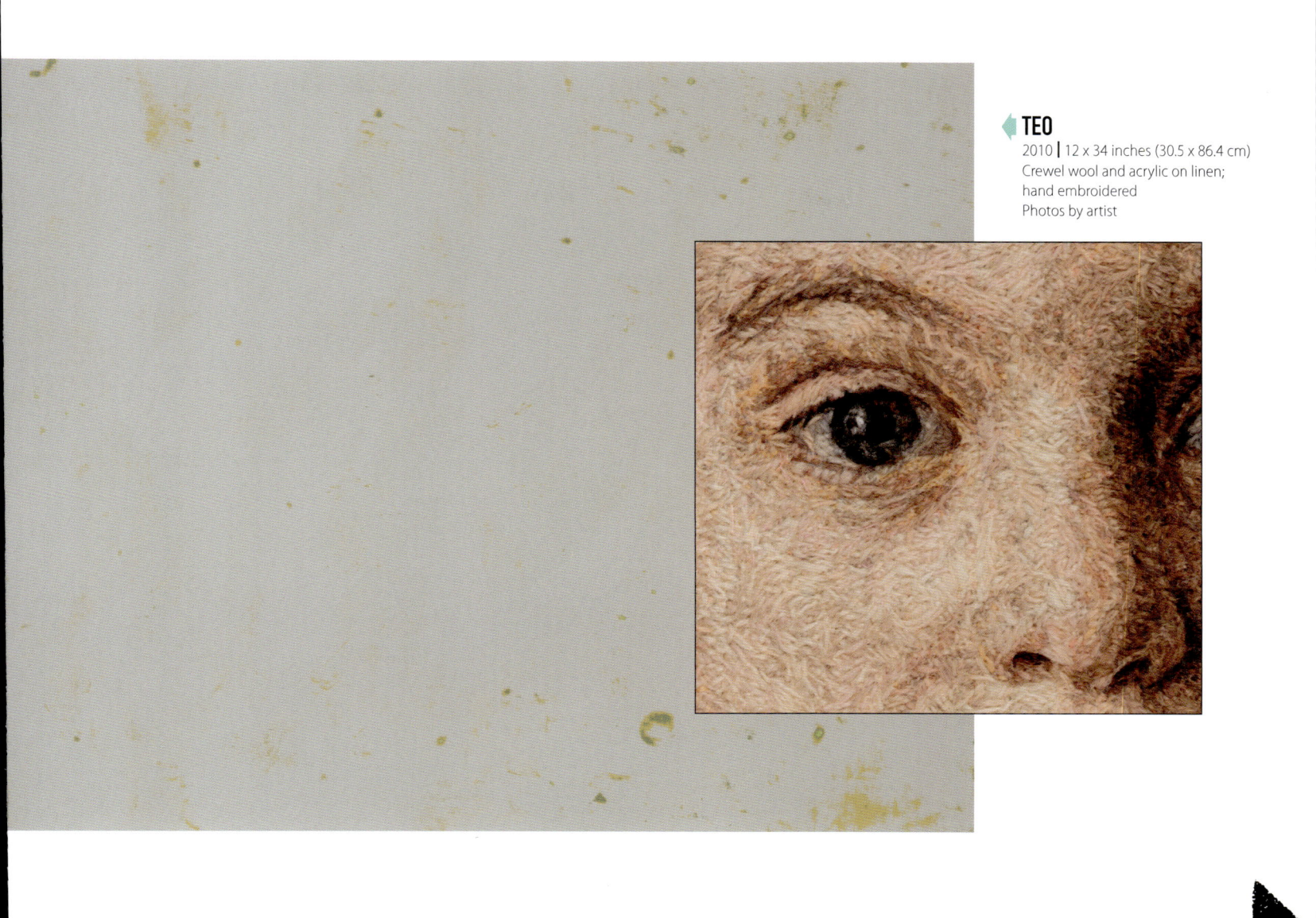

SEVERIJA INČIRAUSKAITĖ-KRIAUNEVIČIENĖ

LITHUANIA

"I create art objects and installations about our lives and realities."

AUTUMN COLLECTION
2007 | Various sizes
Watering can, pail, cover, shredder, cannikin, churn cotton; cross-stitched, drilled
Photo by artist

MORNING TRIO
2009 | 19¹¹⁄₁₆ x 11 x 2⅜ inches
(50 x 28 x 6 cm)
Metal pan, cotton;
cross-stitched, drilled
Photo by artist

Q&A

HOW DO YOU DESCRIBE YOUR WORK? I use uniform embroidery schemes from women's magazines as hallmarks by transferring them onto the lids of aluminum pots, rusty grates, and watering cans, transforming them into objects with an artistic function. **WHY DO YOU USE THIS PARTICULAR COMBINATION OF MATERIALS AND TECHNIQUES?** I had a fascination with everyday objects and found items. Using thread, I have been able to breathe life into objects that are often overlooked or undervalued. I use the concept of kitsch by contrasting the roughness of cheap marketplace art with the homeliness of the urban situation. Each discovery of a new item presents its own challenges and provides another opportunity to explore the world between reality and dreams. My roses, an unoriginal symbol of a woman's everyday life, are, in fact, a cliché. Blossoms on a rusty bucket merging with the bright brown color of metal, or on the lids of huge pots,

DIRECTION
2009 | 13¾ x 8⅝ x 1¹⁵⁄₁₆ inches (35 x 22 x 5 cm)
Metal shovel, cotton; cross-stitched, drilled
Photo by artist

BETWEEN CITY AND VILLAGE
2008 | Various sizes
Metal pail, watering-can, can; cross-stitched, drilled
Photo by artist

turn these nondescript things, although impressive in size, into prestigious objects of desirable interiors.
WHAT INSPIRES YOUR WORK? Moments in daily life, everyday things from our surroundings, pop culture, and kitsch items—all these things inspire me and my art.

WAY OF ROSES
2008 | Car, cotton; cross-stitched, drilled
Photo by artist

◀ **WAY OF ROSES**
2007 | 45¼ x 35⁷⁄₁₆ x 7⅞ inches (115 x 90 x 20 cm)
Car detail, cotton; cross-stitched, drilled
Photo by artist

SEVERIJA INČIRAUSKAITÉ-KRIAUNEVIČIENÉ

CLYDE OLLIVER
ENGLAND

"Stitching into a rigid material like slate means that much of my work could be said to lie somewhere between embroidery and sculpture."

LITTLE KNOT
2008 | 35 13/16 x 9 1/16 x 3 15/16 inches (91 x 23 x 10cm)
Welsh slate, agricultural twine; carved, stitched
Photo by Lucy Barden

DIALOGUE
2006 | 14³⁄₁₆ x 53⅛ x 2¾ inches
(36 x 135 x 7 cm)
Roofing slates; carved, stitched,
assembled on slate shelf
Photo by Lucy Barden

DESCRIBE YOUR WORKING PROCESS. Sometimes I start with a finished form in mind that requires careful sculpting, though more usually I embroider the slate (or occasionally other type of stone) just as I happen to find it. Once I have drilled the slate to allow the passage of needle and thread, I usually use fine linen threads for the stitchery, although on occasion, I will use coarse agricultural twines or rope. The stitches always pass right through the slate, leaving textured marks on the surface reminiscent of Nordic Runes or Ogham script. In other types of work, I will cut channels or grooves in the surface of the slate so that the stitches are countersunk, giving the appearance of fine-line drawings.

This way of working allows me to make representational imagery that appears embedded in the stone.
HOW DID YOU END UP IN THIS PARTICULAR COMBINATION OF MEDIUMS? Although I've always stitched, it wasn't until I was in my forties that I studied textiles seriously. At the time, there was—indeed there still is—a great vogue for making textile work referencing women's lives and histories. I chose instead to look back at working men's histories, and in particular at my father's and grandfather's lives. **HOW MUCH PLANNING DOES IT TAKE TO DO YOUR KIND OF STITCHERY AND WHAT HAVE YOU**

STILL LIFE
2006 | 13 x 9³⁄₁₆ x 1¹⁵⁄₁₆ inches
(33 x 25 x 5 cm)
Slate pieces; embroidered,
assembled on slate shelf
Photo by Lucy Barden

WELSH QUILT
2006 | 37 x 45¹¹⁄₁₆ x 2¾ inches
(94 x 116 x 7 cm)
Slate pieces; embroidered,
assembled on slate shelves
Photo by Lucy Barden

LEARNED ALONG THE WAY? There is no simple answer to this question. Some ideas float around in my head for years and years like an itch that, however hard I try, I just cannot scratch, while other pieces just seem to make themselves. It's often the stone itself that suggests the initial idea to me, so preparing detailed designs before I've found the stone is a waste of time. Having brought the stone back to the studio, I then find that the work tends to take its own path, with me as a kind of concerned onlooker as the work tries to resolve itself (or not). My studio is a litter of half-finished work and broken dreams.

STUDY
2007 | 7 7/16 x 5 7/8 inches (19 x 15 cm)
Slate, some pigmentation, linen stitches; scratched and scribed
Photo by Lucy Barden

LITTLE CAIRN
2010 | 3¹⁵⁄₁₆ x 3⁹⁄₁₆ x 3⁹⁄₁₆ inches (10 x 9 x 9 cm)
Cumbrian slates, sandstone pebble, agricultural twine; pierced
Photo by Lucy Barden

CLYDE OLLIVER

JOETTA MAUE
UNITED STATES

"The images within my work are about personal identity, intimacy, and how identity struggles within the realm of intimacy."

28

AT WORKING THOUGHT
2009 | 75 x 54 inches (190.5 x 137.2 cm)
Re-appropriated linen; hand embroidered, painted
Photo by artist

BREAKS MY HEART
2009 | 14 x 14 inches (35.6 x 35.6 cm)
Re-appropriated linen; hand embroidered
Photo by artist

Q&A

HOW DO YOU DESCRIBE YOUR WORK? My media of embroidery, sewing, knitting, ironing, and folding of linens all come directly out of the home and the role of homemaking. I utilize these tasks and materials to place the work directly into the domain of the home and the female. The viewer can readily identify the conflict being explored in the work while responding to the familiarity of the materials and place in which the work resides. The medium of embroidery innately has detail and precision built into its process. However, as an artist, I do not place importance in that. As a result, my practice is actually very organic and intuitive. Yet I do find the role of beauty very important to my work, and this may at times be expressed through the carefulness of my hand. It is important that my work reveals a love and dedication toward its expression of language or image. Therefore, I am very mindful in the decisions that I make. **HOW DID YOU GET STARTED WITH EMBROIDERY AS A MEDIUM?** I fell into embroidery as an artist. In graduate school, I

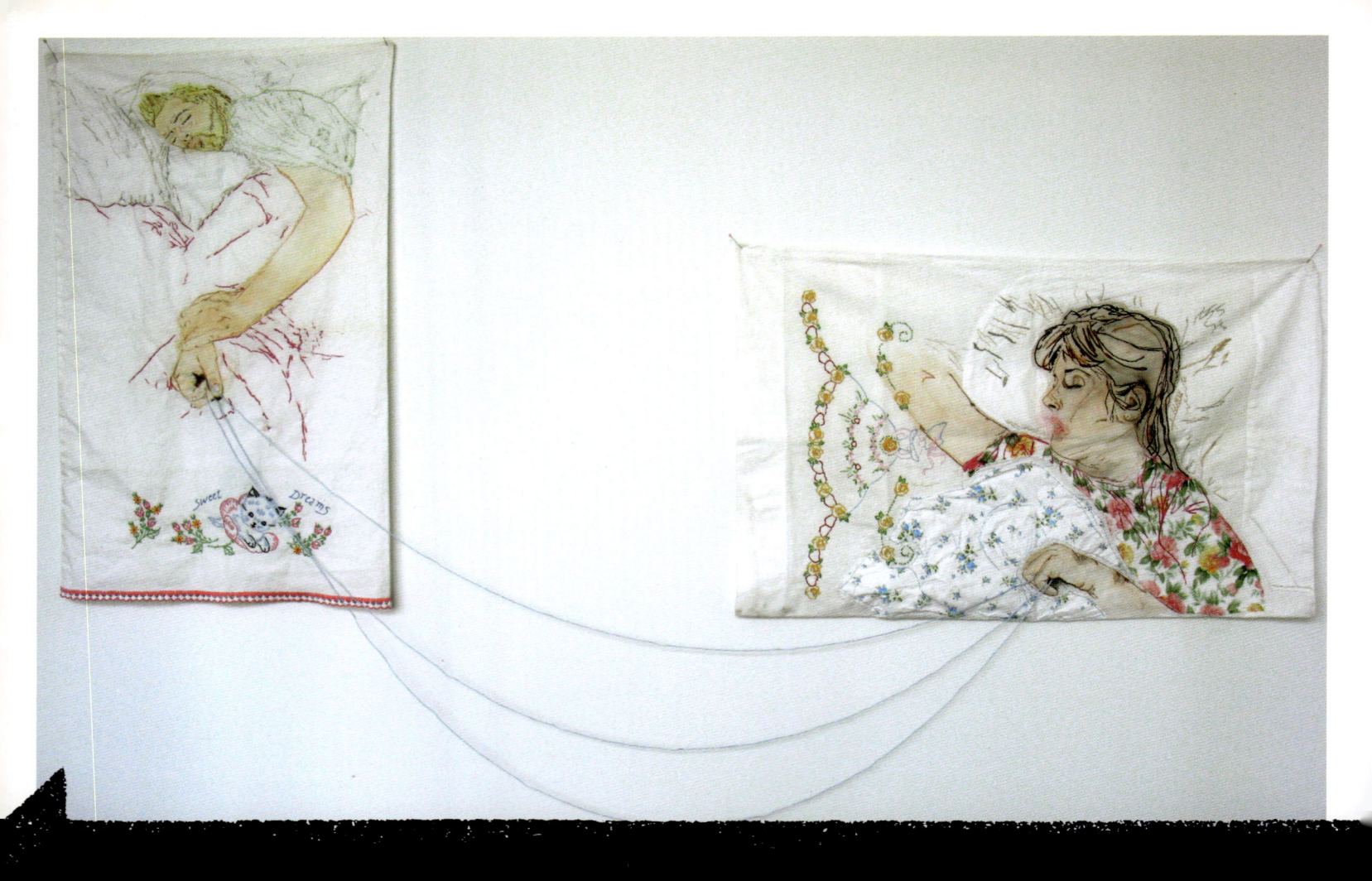

◀ **ASLEEP**
2009 | 67 x 47 inches (170.2 x 119.4 cm)
Re-appropriated linen; hand embroidered, appliqué, painted
Photo by artist

IN WITH YOU ▶
2007 | 30 x 36 x 2 inches (76.2 x 91.4 x 5.1 cm)
Re-appropriated linen with hoop; hand embroidered
Photo by artist

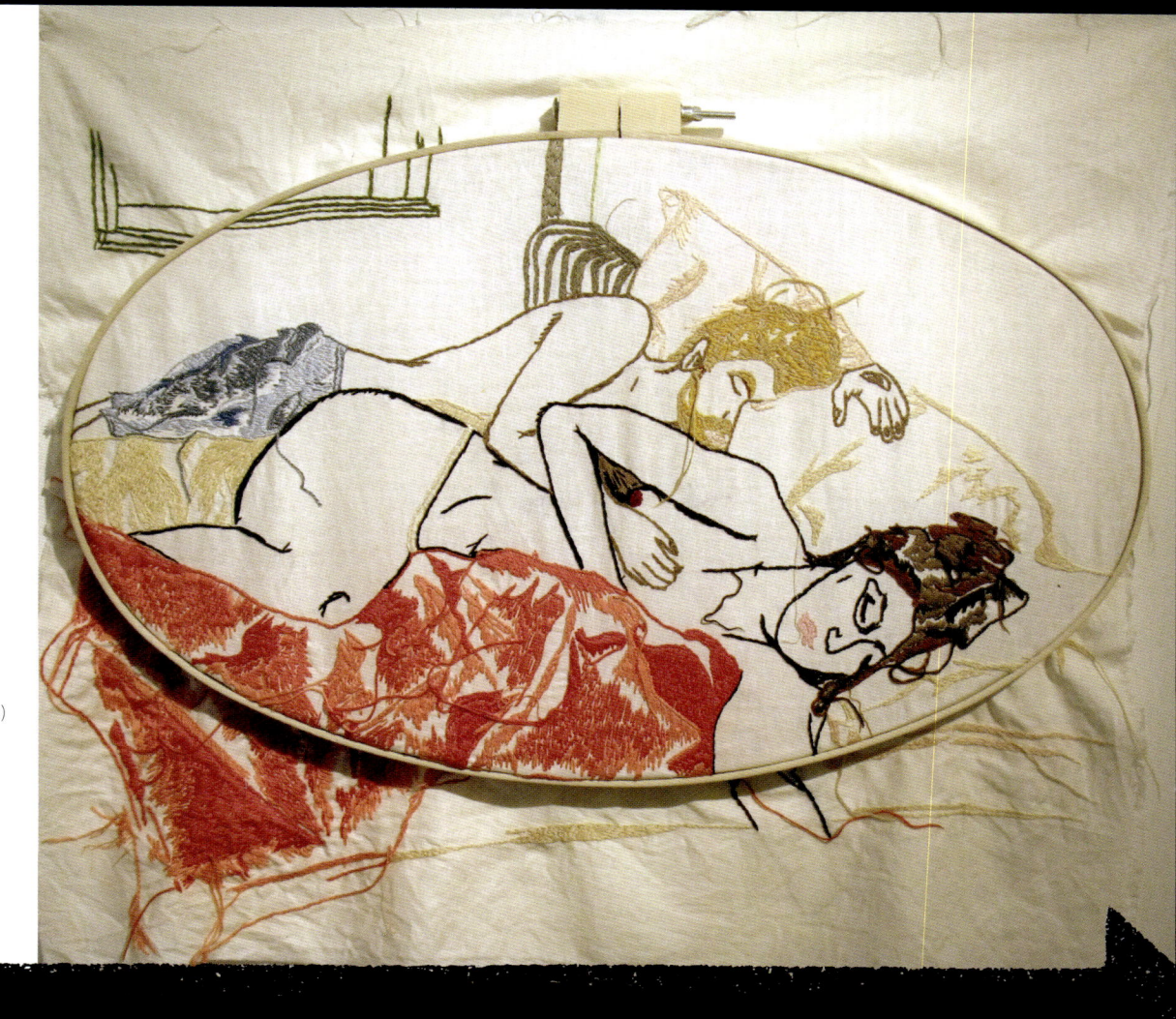

Unexpectedly, I fell in love with the process and medium—so, while simultaneously trying to figure out the next direction for my studio practice and work, I began to explore embroidery as a medium of expression. The medium felt very natural to me as I grew up around fabric and crafts, between my mother and grandmother, and my work had always been made from an overtly feminine point of view. As my new work developed and my love for the process

◀ **WAKING WITH YOU...**
2010 | 80 x 60 x 15 inches
(203.2 x 152.4 x 38.1cm)
Re-appropriated linen, queen-size bed; hand embroidered, appliqué, painted
Photo by artist

of embroidery deepened, I began to enjoy the subversive quality of the medium and how what was expected from a hand-made embroidered piece could be so easily manipulated. **WHERE DO YOU FIND INSPIRATION?** I am most inspired by

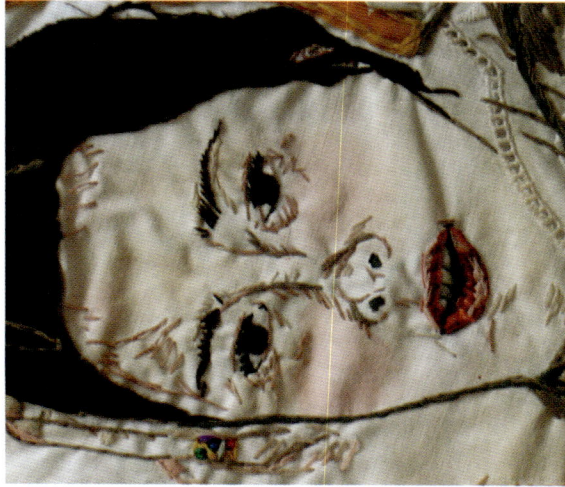

◀ IN BED...
2010 | 29 x 29 inches (73.7 x 73.7 cm)
Re-appropriated linen; hand embroidered, appliqué, painted
Photos by artist

the air as I lie in bed. I am inspired by the complicated, heartbreaking beauty of our daily life and daily intimacy, and this is what I celebrate in my work. With the birth of my first child, a son, I expect to be inspired by him and my new role as a mother as well. I am excited to see how this will affect my work.

ROSIE JAMES
ENGLAND

"My work is stitched drawing. The main focus is on mark making, and I like to compare the different marks you get with printing and stitching."

⬆ **WAITING FOR THE 7:23 TO VICTORIA**
2009 | 18 x 63 inches (46 x 160 cm)
Silk organza, black thread, red embroidery thread; stitched
Photo by artist

HOW DID YOU GET YOUR START IN STITCHERY? I've always had a thing for fabric for as long as I can remember. I think it was watching my mum make stuff from amazing fabrics on her treadle sewing machine. She made some great 70s curtains with a matching seat cover, the color and pattern of which are clearly etched on my brain. That's probably why I have a ridiculous collection of old curtains. When I started out studying textiles, I specialized in print. The stitch was added gradually until it took over, and now print and stitch are nearly equal in consideration. **HAS YOUR SUBJECT MATTER CHANGED OR EVOLVED OVER TIME?** The subject matter started off with images of people out and about, particularly

BERLIN, CHATHAM, PAISLEY
2008 | 31½ x 39⅜ x 1¹⁵⁄₁₆ inches
(80 x 100 x 5 cm)
Black thread, silk, found fabric, cotton;
stitched, screen printed
Photo by artist

crowds in cities, and evolved into focusing on particular groups such as tourists, commuters, art lovers in galleries, etc. I began with just figures and then started to add screen-printed backgrounds or clues to where these people were. Different elements began to appear in my work such as appliquéd fabrics and digitally printed pieces as well as computerized embroidered motifs. But the subject matter is still looking at the individual within the crowd; there

OLYMPIA TOURISTS
2008 | 35 13/16 x 47 5/8 x 1 15/16 inches (91 x 121 x 5 cm)
Silk, linen; machine stitched, screen printed
Photo by artist

are so many crowds. **WHERE DO YOU GATHER INSPIRATION?** Exhibitions, art galleries, museums, doing workshops with all sorts of people and exchanging ideas, blogs…there's so much out there for inspiration. And travel to new and exciting places. And films; I find the Japanese film directors like Ozu and Kurosawa inspiring in the way they use images. I would love to develop some work around film.

PERGAMON LECTURE

2007 | 30½ x 39⅜ x 1¹⁵⁄₁₆ inches (80 x 100 x 5 cm)
Blue thread, silk organza, linen; machine stitched, screen printed
Photos by artist

BUY ONE GET ONE FREE
2009 | 13⅜ x 52¾ x 1¹⁵⁄₁₆ inches (34 x 134 x 5 cm)
Black thread, cotton, silk; machine stitched, screen printed
Photos by artist

ROSIE JAMES

RAQUEL J. ALVES
UNITED KINGDOM

"I like mixing texture. Thus I always use different kinds of paper for my collages. In addition to stitching the lines on paper, I use threads pasted with glue to add movement to my compositions."

40

LUNCH TIME — RED
2009 | 11 13/16 x 9 13/16 x 1 3/16 inches
(30 x 25 x 3 cm)
Photograph-based stitching, watercolor painted paper, threads; pasted on textured paper and canvas
Photo by artist

LUNCH TIME — PURPLE
2009 | 11 13/16 x 9 7/16 x 1 3/16 inches
(30 x 24 x 3 cm)
Photograph-based stitching, watercolor painted paper, threads, tulle; pasted on textured paper and canvas, sewn
Photo by artist

Q&A

DESCRIBE YOUR WORKING PROCESS. My technique is midway between photography—I use a picture as a base—and vector graphic design. Instead of using a digital vectorization tool, I do it manually using needle and thread, adding and manipulating the picture as I see fit. In the same way that I prefer analog photography, I'd rather use traditional techniques applied to a more modern context. **HOW DID YOU DISCOVER YOUR TECHNIQUE?** I have always loved handicrafts, and I started mixing photographs I got from newspapers and magazines. However I did not feel the final product was completely mine. One day I thought I could trace the silhouette of a person from a picture by stitching it to a piece of paper. I liked the outcome, and I thought this could replace the photograph itself. Then I put them on different backgrounds made out of several kinds of paper and added color with watercolors or colored paper. **HAS YOUR PROCESS EVOLVED OVER TIME?** I have more or less "systematized" the work so I will probably needle-paint any picture I like from magazines and newspapers and keep them aside for future collages. Then when I come up with an idea of a composition, I add colors, backgrounds, and everything else, like in a traditional paper collage. Obviously I have

ON THE SPOTLIGHT
2008 | 11¹³⁄₁₆ x 9⁷⁄₁₆ x ½ inches
(30 x 24 x 1.5 cm)
Photograph-based stitching,
watercolor painted paper, threads;
pasted on textured paper and canvas
Photo by artist

ME AND THE CITY
2008 | 9⁷⁄₁₆ x 11³⁄₁₆ x ½ inches (24 x 30 x 1.5 cm)
Photograph-based stitching, watercolor painted
paper, threads; pasted on textured paper and canvas
Photo by artist

some calluses and my hand stitching has improved a lot, not only technically but also in the sense that I am able to give more characteristic details to the subjects I "draw." You have to select the adequate physical features to depict a person with a few lines so they will have the expression you want to convey. **WHAT INSPIRES YOU?** Mostly photography as a way to see the world. Many of the greatest photographs ever taken capture mundane situations, but with the proper approach, they become art.

PENNY NICKELS
UNITED STATES

"I believe that art is the story that the artist is telling the viewer, so in that respect, my work is essentially illustration."

◀ **ZETETIC ASTRONOMY**
2008 | 3½ x 2½ inches (8.9 x 6.4 cm)
Cotton floss, cotton; hand embroidered
Photo by artist

44

FETISH TRIPTYCH: CRONUS, GRAEAE, AND PHORCYDES
2010 | Each: 4 inches (10.2 cm) in diameter
Seeds, elk tooth, urchin, cotton floss on velvet;
hand embroidered, framed in hoops
Photo by artist

IMAGINARY SWATCH
2010 | 6 inches (15.2 cm) in diameter
Seeds, husks, cotton floss, hand-dyed silk;
hand embroidered, framed in hoop
Photo by artist

Q&A

WHAT SUBJECT MATTER DO YOU LIKE TO EXPLORE? Mythological traditions are a theme that I return to over and over again. I've found these stories, despite being antiquated, still have currency today. The postage stamp format is a nod to my printmaking background, as well as being a bit of visual pun. It's a way of celebrating truly famous archetypes and characters. I'm also interested in exploring the roots of needlework. **HOW HAS YOUR TECHNIQUE DEVELOPED OVER TIME?** My embroidery started as an extension of my printmaking. My earliest pieces were my relief prints that I turned into patterns. I've always been planning and executing pieces from that approach, although my stitches have gotten

PENNY NICKELS 45

▲ **KLAUS KINSKI COMMEMORATIVE STAMP**
2009 | 12 inches (30.5 cm) in diameter
Cotton floss, cotton; hand embroidered, framed in hoop
Photo by artist

▲ **ASTERION COMMEMORATIVE STAMP**
2009 | 9 x 12 inches (22.9 x 30.5 cm)
Cotton floss, cotton; hand embroidered
Photo by artist

neater over time. With printmaking, particularly wood block, I was constantly breaking down images into a few steps of light to dark, oversimplifying the gradation. Light and dark grays utilize implied lines. In relief it tends to be hatching and in something like mezzotint, the rocker makes a stipple mark. So for me, stitches like French knots and backstitch are an interpretation of those marks. **WHERE DO YOU FIND INSPIRATION?** Literature always inspires me. I'm

HYPAEPA COMMEMORATIVE STAMP
2009 | 8 x 6 inches (20.3 x 15.2 cm)
Cotton floss, cotton; hand embroidered
Photo by artist

TRITONIS COMMEMORATIVE STAMP
2009 | 9 x 12 inches (22.9 x 30.5 cm)
Cotton floss, cotton; hand embroidered
Photo by artist

currently working on a series exploring the women in Aeschylus' Oresteia. Etymology, too. So many of our words and phrases come directly from fiber. Like "clue," originally "clew," meaning a ball or a ball of string. Specifically the ball of string Daedalus gave Ariadne to guide Theseus out of the labyrinth, creating the first "hint" and giving a new meaning to the word clue. That stuff fascinates me, and I love building pieces around those stories and words.

BASCOM HOGUE
UNITED STATES

"My work is about how cultural and geographical milieus mold the individual psyche and vice versa. My work also explores the ways in which the individual is neither all autonomous nor all a social product."

TWO SATYRS
2010 | 8½ x 10 inches (25.4 x 21.6 cm)
Cotton fabric, polyester thread, cotton batting; freehand sewing machine drawing
Photo by artist

WILLIAM BLAKE
2010 | 10 x 8½ inches (25.4 x 21.6 cm)
Cotton fabric, polyester thread, cotton thread; freehand sewing machine drawing
Photo by artist

Q&A

HOW WOULD YOU DESCRIBE YOUR WORK? I try to make work that is both pleasing to look at and thoughtful. I do not see any hierarchy of arts, which means I give the same amount of attention to anything I make in any medium. My work is at times colorful and at other times monochromatic. My work is about how cultural and geographical milieus mold the individual psyche and vice versa. My work also explores the ways in which the individual is neither all autonomous nor all a social product. My work says do not measure the spiritual worth and social statures of humans by how much one of them owns. **DESCRIBE YOUR START WITH EMBROIDERY.** I learned to sew, and I liked it. Then combining my

BASCOM HOGUE

MODERN TIMES
2009 | 10 x 8 inches (25.4 x 20.3 cm)
Cotton fabric, cotton embroidery floss; hand stitched
Photo by artist

known craft techniques with art just seemed like the next natural step in creativity. I can still make blankets and clothes. **HOW HAS YOUR TECHNIQUE DEVELOPED?** I used to use a few colors and fabrics, and everything was done by hand. I still love handwork. Now when I need to, I will use a sewing machine. And I draw and paint better now than when

BREATHE
2008 | 11½ x 8 inches (29.2 x 20.3 cm)
Cotton fabric, cotton embroidery floss; hand stitched
Photo by artist

I was a child so my designs can be more complicated. **WHAT INSPIRES YOU?** I think every artist should carry their own muse and be inspired first by their own view of things. The quotidian mysteries of daily life mixed up with all the big matters in the world inspire me. **HAVE YOU DEVELOPED ANY NEW TECHNIQUES OR PROCESSES?** No. I use old ways in new ways.

BASCOM HOGUE

GATES OF HELL

2009 | 8 x 11 inches (20.3 x 27.9 cm)
Cotton fabric, cotton embroidery floss;
hand stitched
Photo by artist

JESUS THINKING IN A TREE
2009 | 14 x 11 inches (35.6 x 27.9 cm)
Cotton fabric, cotton batting, cotton embroidery floss; hand stitched
Photo by artist

BASCOM HOGUE

DIEM CHAU
VIETNAM/UNITED STATES

"I work with the mundane and familiar. I like my work to be intimate and have a sense of tactile satisfaction."

LEGACY
2009 | 11½ x 6 x ¾ inches (29.2 x 15.2 x 1.9 cm)
Porcelain plate, silk organza, thread; embroidered, mounted
Photo by artist

▲ **SOJOURN**
2009 | 8 x 8 x ¾ inches (20.3 x 20.3 x 1.9 cm)
Porcelain plate, silk organza, thread; embroidered, mounted
Photo by artist

▲ **SHADOW**
2008 | 4 x 4¾ x 2 inches (10.2 x 12.1 x 5.1 cm)
Porcelain cup, silk organza, thread; embroidered, mounted
Photo by artist

Q&A

HOW DID YOU DEVELOP YOUR TECHNIQUE? I grew up around a lot of sewing and embroidering. My mother was a seamstress and did alterations for extra income. I had the resources around me to explore. Most of what I know I taught myself through trial and error or researching. I like to call it "playing around." **WHAT NEW WORKING PROCESSES HAVE YOU DISCOVERED?** My work constantly evolves. The changes might be very subtle to outside eyes, but I notice them. The newest thing I've done is incorporate colored and patterned fabrics into my embroideries. I think of them as appliqués but applied under the organza instead of on top, like an underglaze in ceramic terms. **WHERE DO YOU FIND INSPIRATION?** Fashion, ethnic textiles, human migration, and our need for identity.

DIEM CHAU

GRASP
2009 | 6½ x 6½ x ¾ inches
(16.5 x 16.5 x 1.9 cm)
Porcelain plate, silk organza, thread;
embroidered, mounted
Photo by artist

WITH OPEN HANDS
2009 | 6 x 6 x ½ inches (15.2 x 15.2 x 1.3 cm)
Porcelain plate, silk organza, thread;
embroidered, mounted
Photo by artist

BLUE DRESS

2009 | 5½ x 5½ x ¾ inches (14 x 14 x 1.9 cm)
Porcelain plate, silk organza, thread; embroidered, mounted
Photo by artist

DIEM CHAU

ORLY COGAN
UNITED STATES

"I often start with vintage linens to which I add my own embroidered drawings and appliqué. The handiwork of stitching, culturally associated with women practitioners and decorating the home, becomes the vehicle for imagery that is run through by the erotic and intimate."

WONDER OF YOU
2007 | 48 x 48 inches (121.9 x 121.9 cm)
Vintage table linen; hand-stitched embroidery, painted
Photo by artist

FORGET ME NOT
2009 | 36 x 36 inches (91.4 x 91.4 cm)
Vintage table linen; hand-stitched embroidery, appliquéd, crocheted, painted
Photos by artist

HOW DID YOU COME TO USE EMBROIDERY IN YOUR ART? I attended a Waldorf School, in which handcrafts and the arts in general were highly regarded, so both were a big part of my school and home life while growing up. Both my parents have a keen eye for antiques. My father had many old figurative paintings in our home that his parents had collected. My mother collected vintage quilts and has a big "sampler" (hand embroidery) collection. I was formerly trained in painting, but I began combining painting, drawing, and embroidery over a decade ago. A few years ago I began doing site-specific installations, and recently I added collage and photography into the mix.

QUANTUM ENTANGLEMENT
(site specific installation)
2009 | 24 x 13 inches (61 x 33 cm)
Mixed media
Photo by artist

HAS YOUR TECHNIQUE CHANGED OVER THE YEARS? It started as small, densely embroidered frolicking figures that played off the patterns on printed fabrics and has evolved into much more complex and elaborate thread drawings, layering imagery that incorporates portraits of actual people in my life. I mix these portraits with fairy tale images on vintage fabrics. When I started working in embroidery, my work began to explore feminist topics and gender issues, which I continue to mine today. **WHAT INSPIRES YOU?** My work has become more personal during these past few years as I have started my own family. Issues of fertility and the nuclear family are creeping into some of my more recent works.

FAIRY TALE
2006 | 90 x 80 inches
(228.6 x 203.2 cm)
Vintage bed sheet; hand-stitched embroidery, painted
Photos by artist

WHAT INFLUENCES YOUR SUBJECT MATTER? I'm telling stories from the influences I see around me in American culture. My work communicates what it feels like for a woman—leading with broad emotional issues like rejection, love, obsession, fear, and desire. The work is arrestingly frank, yet humorous, whimsical, and ironic. Seeing these images sewn upon kitschy vintage table runners is to understand immediately the changes in the tenor of personal expression between then and now. In conflating today's brand of cultural confessionalism with the conservatism of yesteryear, I strive to encapsulate a sweeping arc of feminist history.

ALICIA ROSS
UNITED STATES

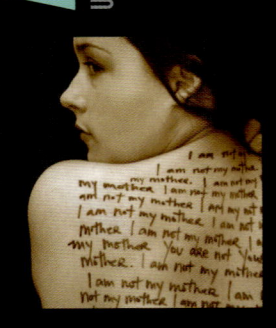

"My work examines contradicting female roles and the simultaneous attraction and repulsion to their objectification."

MOTHERBOARD_7 (SACRED PROFANE)
2008 | 72 x 41 inches
(182.9 x 104.1 cm)
Cotton; cross-stitched
Photo by artist

PHILOSOPHY DEVOURING URANUS
2009 | 27 inches (68.6 cm) in diameter
Cotton; cross-stitched
Photo by artist

Q&A

HOW DID YOU COME TO CHOOSE THIS PARTICULAR MEDIUM? I became frustrated with the limitations of photography, and I have always been interested in sewing and how it relates to feminine identity—historical and contemporary identity. The work evolved from the photographic to fiber, and both media continue to inform the other. **HAS YOUR TECHNIQUE CHANGED OVER TIME?** As a child, I began making quilts and pillows by traditional methods and then as an adult was turned on to using a computerized sewing machine; it has a repetitive, industrial quality that reflects the mass-produced element of pop art that has always fascinated me. The computerized sewing machine also exemplified the digital elements that are important in my work. Ever since I began working in fiber, I have tried to refine the balance between a digital, machine-made aesthetic with handcrafted details. This visual marriage speaks to the feminine dualism between

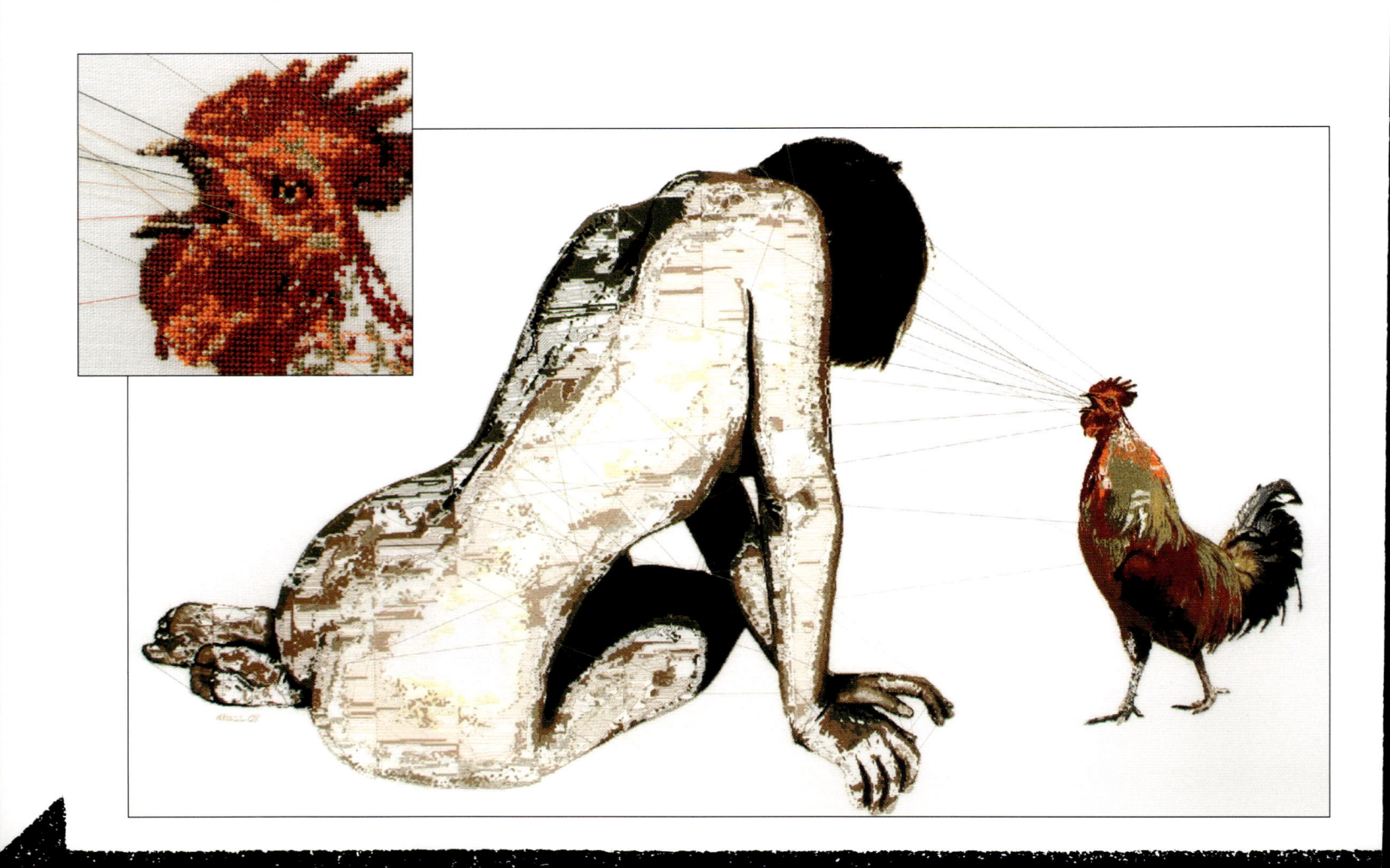

MOTHERBOARD_6
2008 | 41 x 72 inches (104.1 x 182.9 cm)
Cotton; cross-stitched
Photos by artist

PRICK (UN PETIT SOMME D'APRÈS-MIDI)
2008 | 11 x 11 x 4 inches (27.9 x 27.9 x 10.2 cm)
Mixed media
Photos by artist

the woman as homemaker and the woman as object of sexual desire. **WHAT INSPIRES YOU THESE DAYS?** I'm fascinated by popular culture, especially when it involves young women who are scrutinized and shaped by the media. However, I am continually inspired by artists who are not afraid to confront and challenge the viewer.

THANK GOD FOR SCIENCE (OCTOMOM PHRENOLOGY STUDY)
2009 | 40 x 40 inches (101.6 x 101.6 cm)
Cotton; cross-stitched
Photo by artist

PHRENOLOGY STUDY OF DEBRA LAFAVE ▶
2009 | 11 x 14 inches (27.9 x 35.6 cm)
Cotton; cross-stitched
Photo by artist

LUKE HAYNES
UNITED STATES

"I work with quilts. My most recent works investigate nostalgia and function."

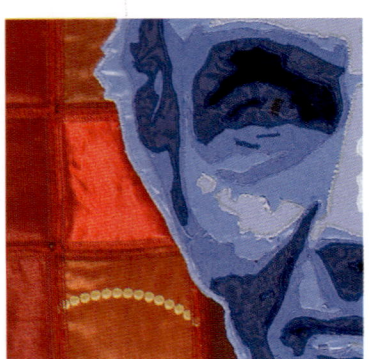

[AMERICAN NOSTALGIA #3] ABRAHAM LINCOLN
2009 | 45 x 75 inches (114.3 x 190.5 cm)
Fabric, batting, thread; quilted
Photos by artist

68

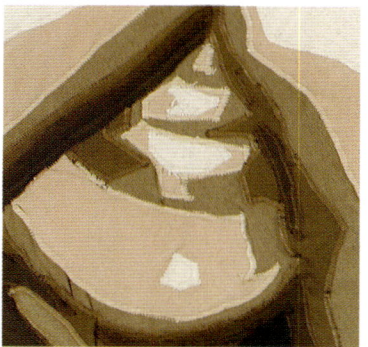

[FRIENDS #5] LAUREN FORD
2008 | 36 x 40 inches (91.4 x 101.6 cm)
Fabric, batting, thread; quilted
Photos by David Papas

Q&A

HOW DID YOU COME TO WORK WITH QUILTS? Quilts are a perfect amalgam of my skills and interests. I have been creating crafts for as long as my motor skills could support them—I guess I never grew out of the friendship bracelet phase of summer camp. I also studied architecture. I am interested in spatial answers to design problems and in creating environments out of planes with the intention of evoking either function or emotion. Every quilt I make teaches me more about the medium. I am continually learning and growing. **WHAT IS UNIQUE ABOUT YOUR WORKING PROCESS?** I have made up everything I do. I bet I have redesigned the wheel several times, when it comes to working methodology.

LUKE HAYNES

[MAN STUFF #1] HAMMER ▶
2007 | 72 x 84 inches (182.9 x 213.4 cm)
Fabric, batting, thread; quilted
Photo by artist

I use computers and photographs to inspire the images of my quilts. **WHERE DO YOU GATHER INSPIRATION?** I am really interested in creating exhibitions and engaging the environment with my works. I have been working in show-sized scale, which allows me to work with larger themes and ideas. I have been bringing in more traditional quilting patterns and methods to my working process—an interesting learning curve. I am continuously inspired by the work of exhibiting artists and contemporary architecture. **WHAT RESPONSES DO YOU GET TO YOUR WORK?** The most common response

[FRIENDS #6] FLAT GLEN
2009 | 70 x 56 inches (177.8 x 142.2 cm)
Fabric, batting, thread; quilted
Photo by artist

is "I have never seen anything like it." That is my favorite, since it shows that I am pushing the boundaries of my medium and getting people to respond to my particular works. My goals with my work are to support myself and create pieces that people remember, to push the boundaries of "quilts" and to explore my creative working method. The more people say that they have been inspired, the more that is accomplished.

[MAN STUFF #4] ELK HEAD
2008 | 45 x 55 inches (114.3 x 139.7 cm)
Fabric, batting, thread; quilted
Photos by David Papas

72

[ICONOGRAPHY #4] REAGAN
2009 | 36 x 55 inches (91.4 x 139.7 cm)
Fabric, batting, thread; quilted
Photo by David Papas

LUKE HAYNES

PETER CRAWLEY
UNITED KINGDOM

"My illustrations use a unique combination of cotton thread and watercolor paper."

74

EMPIRE STATE BUILDING
2009 | 33 1/16 x 23 5/8 inches (84 x 59.7 cm)
420gsm watercolor paper, cotton thread; stitched
Photo by artist

JANUARY
2009 | 11 13/16 x 16 1/2 inches (29.7 x 42 cm)
420gsm watercolor paper,
cotton thread; stitched
Photo by artist

Q&A

DESCRIBE YOUR WORKING PROCESS. Once the illustration has been designed, I prep the paper and pierce it with a pin, often several thousand times. I then stitch cotton thread through the paper, resulting in a textural and engaging, yet minimal, illustration. **HOW DID YOU MAKE YOUR WAY TO THIS PARTICULAR MEDIUM?** The idea of using thread and paper was influenced by nautical route maps, technical drawings, and red-string route markers. After some experimentation, the final combination of watercolor paper, cotton thread, red cross-stitch thread, and letterpress typography gave me the desired texture while retaining a minimal feel. **HOW HAS YOUR TECHNIQUE EVOLVED?** After each illustration, I learn

PETER CRAWLEY

MOUNTAIN

2010 | 16½ x 11¹³⁄₁₆ inches (42 x 29.7 cm)
420gsm watercolor paper, cotton thread; stitched
Photos by artist
Designed by Peter Crawley and Ben O'Brien

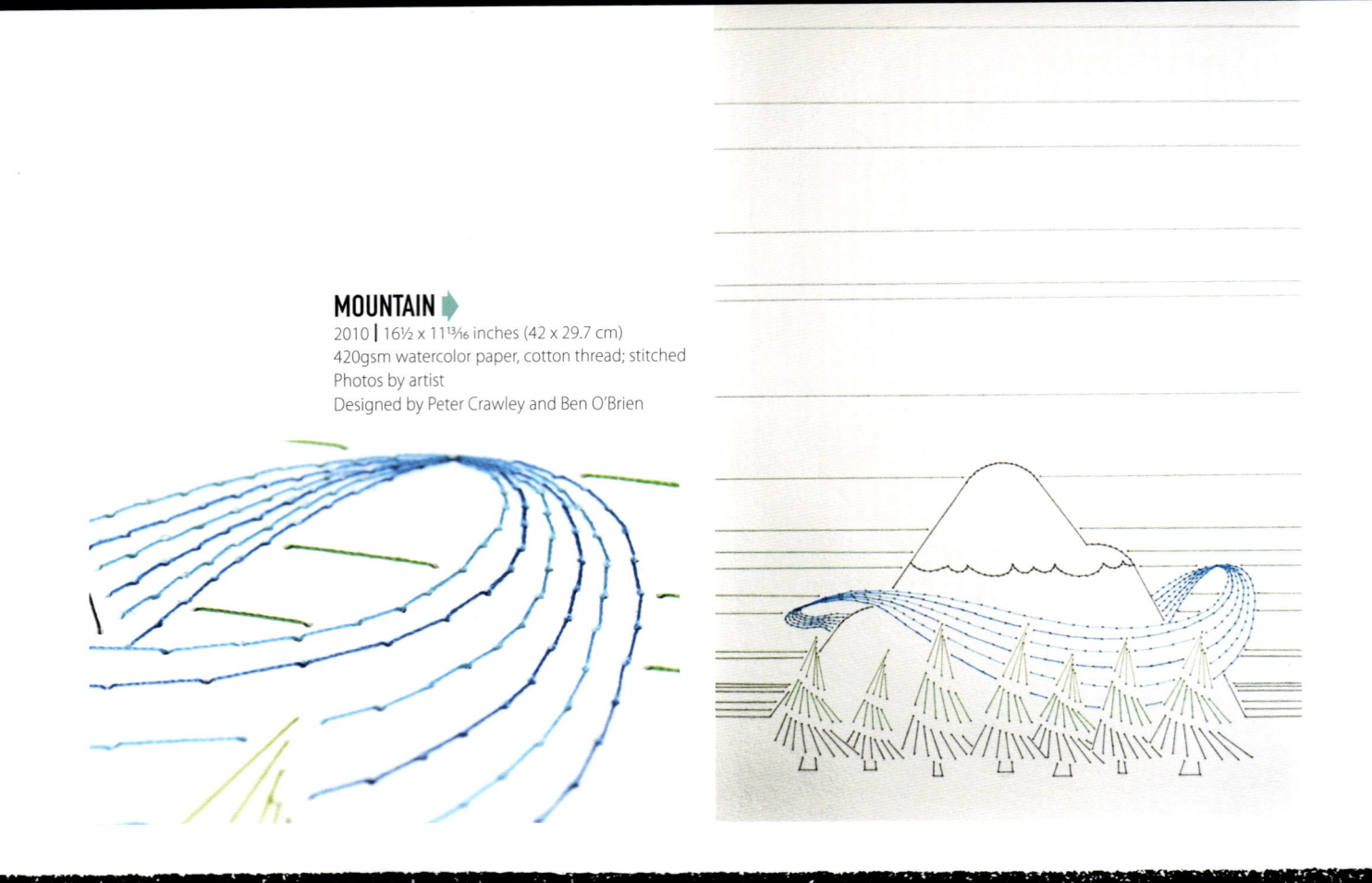

more about the materials and how to manipulate them. The materials are unforgiving so patience is very important. The technique is actually very simple but relies on a great deal of accuracy when piercing the paper. **HOW MUCH PLANNING DO YOUR PIECES REQUIRE?** Stitched illustrations take a lot of planning; every hole must be perfectly aligned to ensure the lines are parallel when stitched. Lines of perspective in buildings, and parallel lines in typography require careful planning to ensure they do not appear out of place or misaligned. The larger architectural illustrations in particular benefit from a good deal of planning. The most important lesson learned from the illustrations to date

◀ **BBC BROADCASTING HOUSE**
2009 | 35 x 23⅝ inches (59.7 x 42 cm)
420gsm watercolor paper,
cotton thread; stitched
Photo by artist

is quite simply that patience really is a virtue. A few extra minutes concentrating on the preparation and stitching of an illustration can really make it stand out from a rushed piece. **WHERE DO YOU DRAW INSPIRATION?** Being a product designer is a constant source of inspiration, though sources of inspiration as both product designer and illustrator often overlap. The built environment, good design, and geometry constantly provide me with inspiration.

TILLEKE SCHWARZ
NETHERLANDS

"I stitch 'maps of modern life' that remind [the viewer] of graffiti."

PLAYGROUND

2008 | 21⅝ x 20¹/₁₆ inches
(55 x 51 cm)
Threads on linen;
hand embroidered
Photos by Rob Mostert

Q&A

HOW DO YOU DESCRIBE YOUR WORK AND YOUR SUBJECT MATTER? I include anything that moves, amazes, or intrigues me. Daily life, mass media, traditional samplers, and cats are major sources of inspiration. The result is a mixture of content, graphic quality, and fooling around. The work can be understood as a kind of visual poetry. **DOES YOUR WORK CONTAIN AN UNDERLYING NARRATIVE?** The work contains narrative elements. Not really complete stories, with a beginning, a storyline, and an end. On the contrary, the narrative structures are used as a form of communication with the viewer. The viewer is invited to decipher connections or to create them. The viewer may assemble the stories and produce chronological and causal structures. Actually, the viewer might step into the role of the author. It can become a kind of play between the viewer and the artist. **HOW DID YOU GET STARTED WITH STITCHERY?** I learned to stitch as a child and always

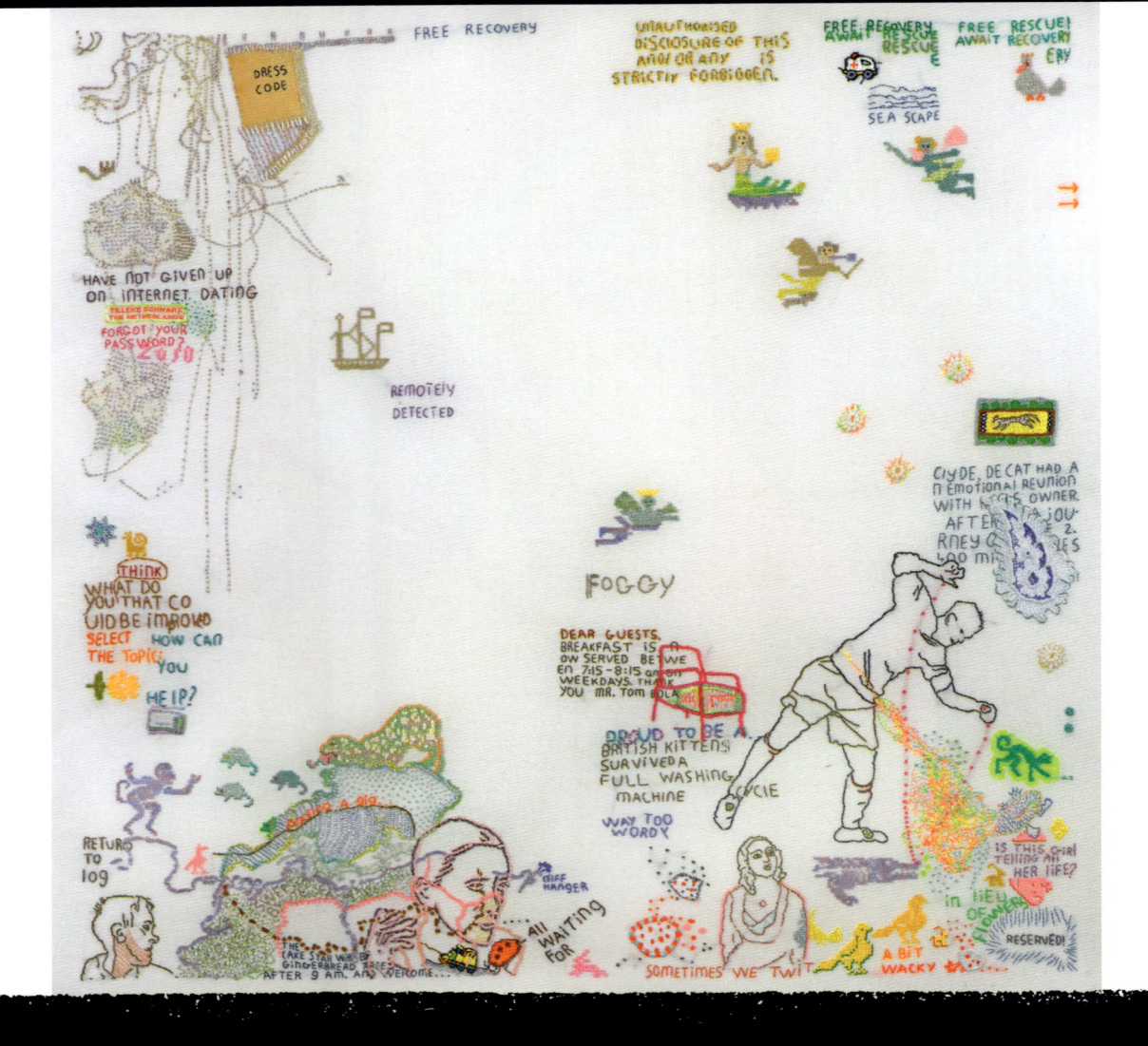

FREE RECOVERY

2010 | 26 x 26¾ inches (66 x 68 cm)
Threads on linen; hand embroidered
Photos by Rob Mostert

loved it. During my art education in drawing I used to stitch at home. I love textiles because of their tactile nature. Textiles generally have a more intimate relationship with the viewer and are very suitable for communicating emotions.
HAVE YOU DEVELOPED ANY NEW WORKING PROCESSES? Not really. My interest is in the content and not the technique.

WELCOME TO THE REAL WORLD
2001 | 26¾ x 26 inches (68 x 66 cm)
Threads on linen; hand embroidered
Photos by Rob Mostert

IF

2009 | 28 5/16 x 24 3/8 inches (72 x 62 cm)
Threads on linen; hand embroidered
Photos by Rob Mostert

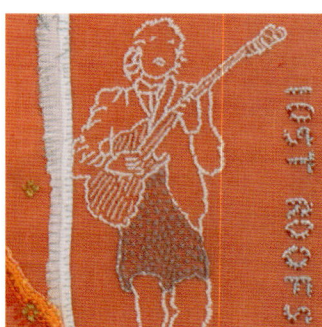

JENNIFER BOE
UNITED STATES

"I do my work in series of no more than 15. Each series is a cataloging or listing of like objects."

84

◀ IMMACULATE MARY FULL OF GRACE
2005-2006 | 60 x 50 inches (152.4 x 127 cm)
Found linen tablecloth; embroidered
Photo by artist

ALWAYS SAVE VS. PHILIP MORRIS ▶
2007 | 36 x 14 inches each (91.4 x 35.6 cm each)
Found linen runners; embroidered
Photo by artist

Q&A

HOW DO YOU DESCRIBE THE WORK THAT YOU DO? I do my work in series of no more than 15. Each series is a cataloging or listing of like objects (i.e. images of gay porn, images of lesbian porn, forms of birth control, things one might find in a woman's purse, sandwiches, cuts of beef, bars of soap, religious icons). **HOW DID YOU GET YOUR START IN THIS PARTICULAR MEDIUM?** I graduated in 2001 from the Kansas City Art Institute with a BFA in Painting and Creative Writing. At that time I did narrative paintings. After I graduated, due to a lack of dedicated studio space, my paintings went from being measured in feet to being measured in inches. And, because they were smaller, I turned them out faster and

JENNIFER BOE

▲ **RIB ROAST, $7.99LB**
2009 | 32 x 32 inches (81.3 x 81.3 cm)
Flour sack towel; embroidered, transferred
Photo by artist

▲ **BEEF BRISKET, $3.19LB**
2009 | 32 x 32 inches (81.3 x 81.3 cm)
Flour sack towel; embroidered, transferred
Photo by artist

eventually even without thought. My apartment became a slagheap of meaningless little paintings and for the first time, instead of asking myself why I made art, I asked myself why I painted. I knew why I made art, but I didn't know why I painted, so I stopped. In 2002, Erin Zona, a fellow graduate of KCAI, showed an embroidered piece in the exhibition Art for the Masses at the now defunct Dirt Gallery in the West Bottoms of Kansas City. The embroidery was cut in the shape of Texas, as was the frame, and, being Texas, it was huge. It was and is something beyond amazing, and I thought I could do better. **HAS YOUR TECHNIQUE DEVELOPED OR CHANGED OVER TIME?** When I started, I just did small

HOLIDAY TURKEY
2004 | 32 x 36 inches (81.3 x 91.4 cm)
Found cotton tablecloth; embroidered
Photos by artist

line drawings, like those in the Hanky Panky series, with an outline stitch. Then, I had this ambitious idea to embroider a hog's head, and that's how I stumbled upon the couching stitch and French knots; those are the main stitches I use now. I also came to realize that thread is a three-dimensional object, and it produces its own shading to a degree. **WHAT WORDS OF WISDOM WOULD YOU SHARE WITH PEOPLE WHO WANT TO TRY YOUR MEDIUM?** One hundred wrongs make a right. As long as you are consistent, nobody can tell that you are doing it "wrong." That goes for all forms of needlecraft and most any other process, with the exception of those involving acids and combustibles, for obvious reasons.

◀ **ARTIST'S STANDARD**
2003 | 84 x 70 inches (213.4 x 177.8 cm)
Silk; embroidered
Photos by artist

⬆ LET THEM EAT CAKE
2004 | 36 x 36 inches (91.4 x 91.4 cm)
Flour sack; embroidered, transferred
Photos by artist

GILLIAN BATES
UNITED KINGDOM

"I produce contemporary textile art in the form of wall-hung canvases."

BEACH HUTS
2009 | 14 x 14 inches (35.6 x 35.6 cm)
New, vintage, and reclaimed fabrics; appliqué, machine embroidered
Photos by artist

MERMAID STREET
2010 | 14 x 14 inches (35.6 x 35.6 cm)
New, vintage, and reclaimed fabrics; appliqué, machine embroidered
Photos by artist

HOW DO YOU DESCRIBE YOUR WORK AND YOUR MATERIALS? All of my handmade canvases are entirely unique and are created using reclaimed and vintage fabrics. With levels of care and attention that only come from focused obsession, I work in a fantastically wide range of canvas sizes and colors. Recently I have felt more and more compelled to explore and celebrate my local environment. The brilliantly idiosyncratic seaside town of Sussex, its wonderful residents, and stunning architecture continue to be the single greatest driving force behind my work and a constant source of enjoyment and inspiration. **WHY DO YOU CHOOSE TO WORK WITH RECLAIMED MATERIALS?** Whether they be found, donated, or

▲ **THE BOWLERS**
2010 | 10 x 12 inches (25.4 x 30.5 cm)
New, vintage, and reclaimed fabrics;
appliqué, machine embroidered
Photo by artist

purchased at the charity store, reclaimed fabrics have obvious environmental and economic benefits for me as an artist. The reclaimed fabrics hold a deeper resonance for me, though. These old clothes, once worn and treasured, had been let go, and now, through my work, they find new life. Their old stitches are torn apart only for new ones to

BRIGHTON PROMENADE
2010 | 18 x 18 inches (45.7 x 45.7 cm)
New, vintage, and reclaimed fabrics;
appliqué, machine embroidered
Photo by artist

old artifacts, I aim to explore the relationship of then and now. In doing so, I hope to gain fresh insights into past lives and present. **WHERE DO YOU FIND INSPIRATION?** I believe that habit and habitat draw a veil over our eyes. We become so accustomed to the people and places we see every day that eventually we fail to see them properly at all. My aim is to pull back the veil, and in doing so, reveal the extraordinary and beautiful wonder of everyday life.

🔺 **THE PROMENADERS**
2010 | 14 x 18 inches (35.6 x 45.7 cm)
New, vintage, and reclaimed fabrics;
appliqué, machine embroidered
Photo by artist

🔺 **END OF THE PIER**
2010 | 18 x 16 inches (45.7 x 40.6 cm)
New, vintage, and reclaimed fabrics;
machine embroidered
Photo by artist

WELCOME TO EASTBOURNE PIER
2010 | 12 x 23½ inches (30.5 x 59.7 cm)
New, vintage, and reclaimed fabrics;
machine embroidered
Photo by artist

JENNIFER L. PORTER
UNITED STATES

"As I create, the Jungian archetype subtly dictates a psychical cohesiveness: the artist becomes a transcriber of the portentous, and simultaneously, the viewer becomes increasingly important."

96

BLACK SWAN

2009 | 12 x 12 x 2 inches
(30.5 x 30.5 x 5.1 cm)
Vintage and new embroidery floss on muslin; hand embroidered
Photo by Jay Dawes

HOUSE PERSON TREE

2009 | 12 x 12 x 2 inches
(30.5 x 30.5 x 5.1 cm)
Vintage and new embroidery floss on muslin; hand embroidered
Photo by Light Box Bacon

Q&A

WHAT DREW YOU TO EMBROIDERY? I am fond of intricacy. My background in photography and video became less enticing as the prevalence of a digital reality began to dictate the flow of their respective arts. Embroidery is intricate. And demanding. And will not suffer from the lack of courtesy afforded my other art forms of choice. **HAS YOUR APPROACH TO THE MEDIUM CHANGED OVER TIME?** My love for the textural—for the pure feel—was something that was mostly self-cultivating. The more I saw, and the more I filtered, the more enmeshed I became in a realm of creativity that I felt, in its timelessness, I could be comfortable in for the long haul. Simply, I could see myself changing it while

JENNIFER L. PORTER

SAND PLAY (TOURNIQUET) ▶
2009 | 12 x 12 x 2 inches
(30.5 x 30.5 x 5.1 cm)
Vintage and new embroidery
floss on muslin; hand embroidered
Photo by Lisa Weiner

it remained steadfast. Beautiful and stubborn. **HOW HAS YOUR SUBJECT MATTER EVOLVED?** The more I delve into my own shadow, the more complex the work becomes. I believe that our personal shadows hold a rich source of information about ourselves, and the key is not to judge what we discover once we shine the light on it. Beautiful jewels are hiding in there, and I hope my work will reflect my discoveries. **WHAT INSPIRES YOU THESE DAYS?** Today, the sweet simplicity

PRICILLA WAITS FOR DRIER TIMES

2009 | 12 x 12 x 2 inches (30.5 x 30.5 x 5.1 cm)
Vintage and new embroidery floss on muslin;
hand embroidered
Photos by Lisa Weiner

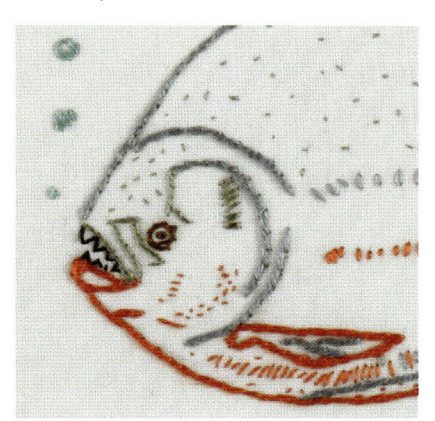

of feeding my cat, watering the herbs in my kitchen, the tiny joy of writing these sentences knowing (hoping) that someone heretofore untouched by the unstable wackiness of the "art versus craft" debate may be gently swept up into its fleeting tide.

GOING ON EMPTY HANDED

2009 | 24 x 24 x 2 inches (61 x 61 x 5.1 cm)
Vintage and new embroidery floss on muslin; hand embroidered
Photos by Aaron Maloof

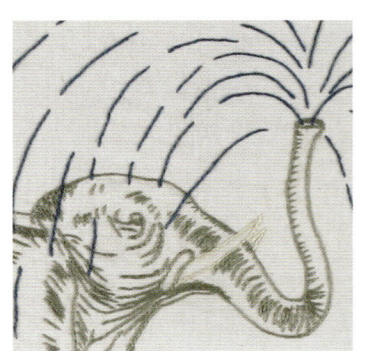

100

◀ **HILL DRIVER**
2010 | 12 x 12 x 2 inches (30.5 x 30.5 x 5.1 cm)
Vintage and new embroidery floss on muslin; hand embroidered
Photos by Eric Singley

JENNIFER L. PORTER 101

CHARLENE MULLEN
UNITED KINGDOM

"I am best known for my way of using blackwork embroidery with modern iconography. It is the combination of recreating London landscapes and their illustrative design that appeals to people."

THE GHERKIN
2009 | 17 x 17 inches (43.2 x 43.2 cm)
100% wool; hand embroidered
Photo by Rachel Smith

ITALY ▶

2009 | 14³⁄₁₆ x 23⅝ inches (36 x 60 cm)
100% wool; hand embroidered
Photo by Rachel Smith

Q&A

HOW DID YOU ARRIVE AT EMBROIDERY AS A MEDIUM? I trained in textiles for my BA and Illustration (Royal College of Art) so my fashion work often was combined with very illustrative work. I taught myself embroidery, and I love how it can replicate a drawn line. But the sewn medium makes it much more special, and I like the process of the sewing. Nothing is identical. **WHERE DO YOU FIND INSPIRATION?** I love typography and maps, including more quirky views of London as well as ways to show what is unique about that landscape and how to interpret that in stitching. I loved the quilt

LONDON CALLING PARIS
2009 | 14³⁄₁₆ x 47¼ inches (36 x 120 cm)
100% wool; hand embroidered
Photo by Rachel Smith

show at the Victoria & Albert Museum, early slipware by Thomas Toft, Swiss paper cuts, and replicating crochet patterns in stitching. **HOW HAS YOUR TECHNIQUE DEVELOPED?** I don't know if it has! I have to really like what I want to draw, and though I have made some scenes from an amalgamation of buildings, I much prefer to actually go and draw

JAPAN
2009 | 14³⁄₁₆ x 23⅝ inches (36 x 60 cm)
100% wool; hand embroidered
Photo by Rachel Smith

the landscape and edit as I go along. **WHAT RESPONSES DO YOU GET TO YOUR WORK?** People are drawn to the work, because they are often familiar with a scene and like to see how I have interpreted it in stitching. Hidden in the pattern are touches of humor, which I like to think people discover with time.

⬆ **THE GHERKIN & TOWER BRIDGE**
2008 | 14 3/16 x 35 7/16 inches (36 x 90 cm)
100% wool; machine embroidered
Photo by Rachel Smith

⬆ **LITTLE RED BUS**
2008 | 14 3/16 x 35 7/16 inches (36 x 90 cm)
100% wool; machine embroidered
Photo by Rachel Smith

▲ OXO & QUEEN ELIZABETH HALL
2008 | 14³⁄₁₆ x 23⅝ inches (36 x 60 cm)
100% wool; hand embroidered
Photo by Rachel Smith

CHARLENE MULLEN

MARLOES DUYKER
NETHERLANDS

"An infinite fusion between fine art, poetry, and fashion."

GOLDFISH
2005 | 12⁹⁄₁₆ x 9⁷⁄₁₆ inches (32 x 24 cm)
Linen, paper, organza, yarn;
appliqué, free motion embroidery
Photo by Norbert Waalboer

VOLVO
2009 | 7⅞ x 10¼ inches (20 x 26 cm)
Linen, yarn, lace; appliqué,
free motion embroidery
Photo by artist

Q&A

HOW DID YOU GET YOUR START IN STITCHERY? During my study at the School of Arts in Utrecht, I was encouraged to experiment with all kinds of unconventional materials, since illustrating is much more than a pencil drawing or a painting. One day my mother had been using the sewing machine, and I saw what could be an interesting device to make images. The created images were very fragile, both abstract and figurative, a refreshing and exciting new approach to create an image: using the sewing machine as a pencil. **WHAT INSPIRES YOU AND YOUR WORK?** I often go out, armed with my camera to capture inspiration. Nature is an endless source of inspiration. I can get carried away by ruins, molds,

MARLOES DUYKER

◆ **SWEET GUNS**
2006 | 10¼ x 8⅝ inches (26 x 22 cm)
Linen, paper; appliqué,
free motion embroidery
Photo by artist

moss, and decay—the way nature transforms everything. Momentarily, I'm working with weathered materials and tree bark. I also love fashion, architecture, purity, humor, and cocky people. **HAS YOUR SUBJECT MATTER SHIFTED AT ALL?** The work has become more conceptual, minimal, and subtle, criticizing topics like overconsumption and artificial

110

◀ **CAPRICORN**
2006 | 13⅜ x 10¼ inches (34 x 26 cm)
Cotton wick, yarn, paper, sewing
machine; appliqué,
free motion embroidery
Photo by artist

beauty. Sometimes it's the exact opposite, and I just feel like creating beautiful birds. **HOW HAVE YOUR TECHNIQUES AND PROCESSES DEVELOPED?** It is the medium that has evolved mostly, from canvas to an actual product like furniture to fashion, and jewelry. Joining forces and working with other designers is another important development.

◀ **LADY IN RED**
2008 | 14³⁄₁₆ x 7⅞ inches (36 x 20 cm)
Cotton, yarn, lace; appliqué,
free motion embroidery
Photos by artist

LENNON
2006 | 11⅘ x 9⅘ inches (30 x 25 cm)
Various fabrics and textiles, yarn, printed paper; appliqué, free motion embroidery
Photo by artist

CÉCILE JARSAILLON

FRANCE

"I sew over images with cotton thread; the original image disappears, leaving only hatching."

L'ENFANT ET LES PRODUITS
2009 | 5⅞ x 5⅞ inches (15 x 15 cm)
Photographs; embroidered
Photo by artist

CHEZ LE BOUCHER
2009 | 9¹³⁄₁₆ x 7⅞ inches (25 x 20cm)
Photographs; embroidered
Photo by artist

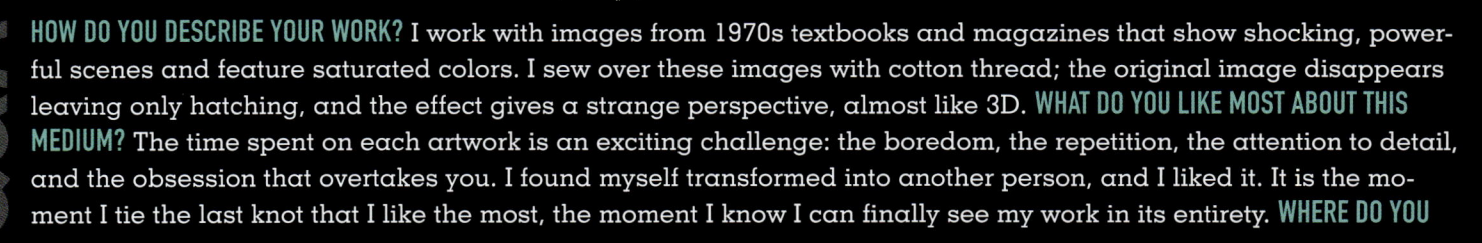

HOW DO YOU DESCRIBE YOUR WORK? I work with images from 1970s textbooks and magazines that show shocking, powerful scenes and feature saturated colors. I sew over these images with cotton thread; the original image disappears leaving only hatching, and the effect gives a strange perspective, almost like 3D. **WHAT DO YOU LIKE MOST ABOUT THIS MEDIUM?** The time spent on each artwork is an exciting challenge: the boredom, the repetition, the attention to detail, and the obsession that overtakes you. I found myself transformed into another person, and I liked it. It is the moment I tie the last knot that I like the most, the moment I know I can finally see my work in its entirety. **WHERE DO YOU**

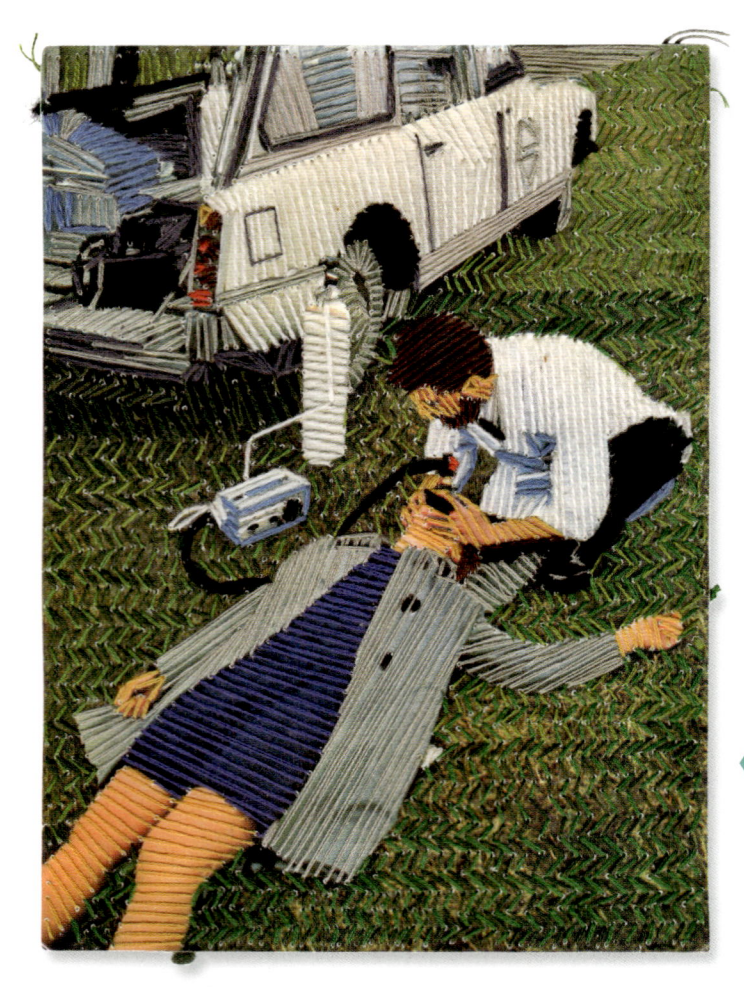

◀ **LA FEMME INANIMEE**
2009 | 7⅞ x 3¹⁵⁄₁₆ inches (20 x 10 cm)
Photographs; embroidered
Photo by artist

FIND INSPIRATION? The things that interest me are shock, sex, violence, love, laughter, absurdity, beauty, and contrasts. There is enough inspiration within our contemporary world. Every day, I want to tell something new, share my views through art. **TELL US ABOUT YOUR SUBJECT MATTER.** I'm currently looking for other themes. I am only at the beginning of

▲ **LES ENFANTS ET LE SANG**
2009 | 3¹⁵⁄₁₆ x 5⅞ inches (10 x 15 cm)
Photographs; embroidered
Photo by artist

my work in embroidery, because I did more painting until now. With embroidery, I am plunged into a strange world, thanks to the incredible people I have met—Art Brut artists, prisoners—who also use the same medium with such creativity and imagination. It motivates me to explore my art even further.

EMILY EIBEL
UNITED STATES

"I make narrative stitchings and illustrations constructed with a combination of appliqué and embroidered drawing."

ROADKILL STEW
2009 | 11 x 9 inches
(27.9 x 22.9 cm)
Fabric, thread; appliqué,
machine stitched
Photos by artist

NIGHT WATCHMAN
2008 | 9 x 9 x ¾ inches
(22.9 x 22.9 x 1.9 cm)
Fabric, thread; appliqué,
machine stitched
Photo by artist

U&A

HOW DID YOU GET STARTED WITH STITCHERY AS A MEDIUM? While studying illustration at Pratt Institute, we were encouraged to experiment with many media. A friend and I decided to play around with fabric, appliqué, and embroidery. I really ended up enjoying it, and I guess it stuck! **HAS YOUR TECHNIQUE CHANGED OVER TIME?** My first several pieces used many more stitches than I use today. I've found that my imagery and line quality benefit from as clean a stitch as possible. It also helps that I don't use embroidery thread. I've found I get a finer line from sewing thread. **HOW HAS YOUR SUBJECT MATTER EVOLVED?** When I first began, I approached all my pieces as conceptual one-liners. Now I'm just interested in

▲ **BUTTERFACE**
2008 | 5 x 5 x ½ inches (12.7 x 12.7 x 1.3 cm)
Fabric, thread, panel; appliqué,
machine stitched
Photo by artist

▲ **FRESHLY BUTCHERED MEAT**
2008 | 11¾ x 9 inches (29.8 x 22.9 cm)
Fabric, thread, panel; appliqué,
machine stitched
Photo by artist

making playful work that means something to me. **WHAT INSPIRES YOUR WORK?** I'm inspired by narrative. Each stitching begins in my mind as a story or a scene. Nature is also a big inspiration. That may be because I miss it now that I'm living in the city! **WHAT NEW TECHNIQUES OR TIPS HAVE YOU DISCOVERED?** I think each new stitching becomes a little easier

▲ STILL FACE
2009 | 6 x 6 x ½ inches (15.2 x 15.2 x 1.3 cm)
Fabric, thread, panel;
appliqué, machine stitched
Photo by artist

and a little quicker. I highly suggest basting (if you use appliqué), fusible interfacing (to keep fraying fabrics under control), and stretching your finished pieces on a board rather than stretcher bars or embroidery rings (on which the fabric can become loose or punctured).

DOWNRIGHT
2007 | 9 x 9 x ¾ inches
(22.9 x 22.9 x 1.9 cm)
Fabric, thread; appliqué,
machine stitched
Photo by artist

▲ **HEY COURBET!**
2009 | 8 x 8 inches (20.3 x 20.3 cm)
Fabric, thread; appliqué
Photo by artist

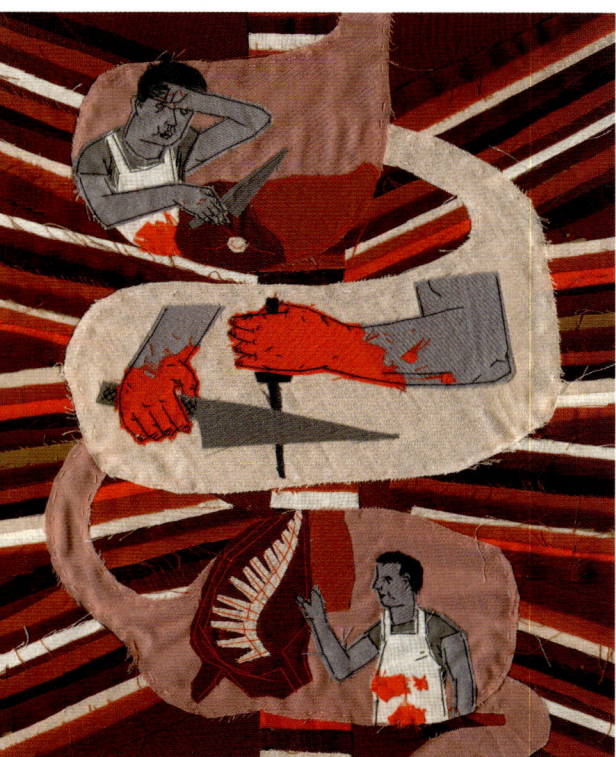

▲ **BUTCHER**
2008 | 10¼ x 8¼ x ¾ inches (26 x 21 x 1.9 cm)
Fabric, thread, matte medium; appliqué, machine stitched
Photo by artist

EMILY EIBEL 123

WILLIAM SCHAFF
UNITED STATES

"In the case of my embroidery, it is just that: hand-embroidered images—some of a religious nature, some of a decorative nature, and some of an expressionistic nature."

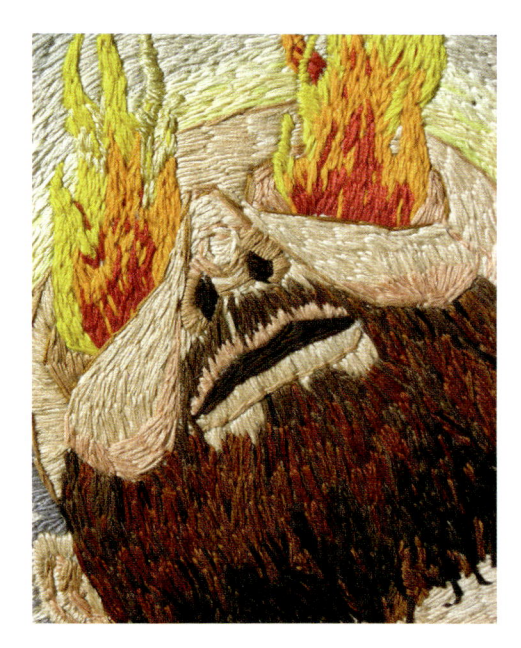

◀ **WHAT IS HUMAN?**
2007–2008 | 20½ x 16½ inches (52.1 x 41.9 cm)
Cotton thread, white cotton; hand embroidered
Photos by artist

◀ **UNDER THE QUICKSAND**
2007 | 9 x 8½ inches (22.9 x 21.6 cm)
Cotton thread, black cotton; hand embroidered
Photo by artist

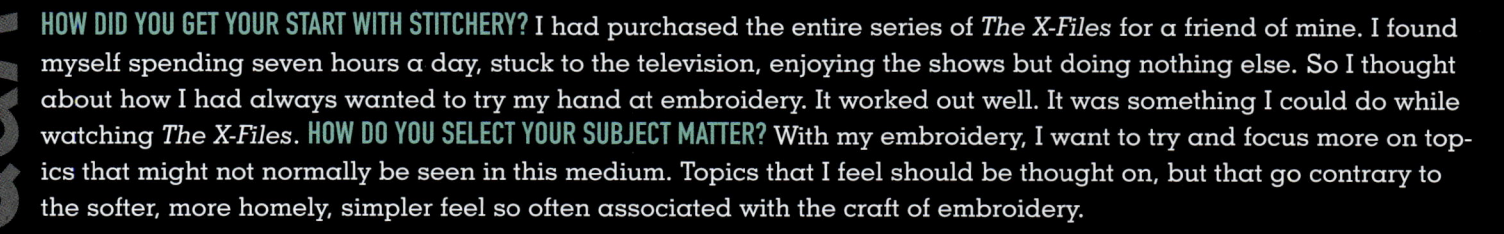

Q&A

HOW DID YOU GET YOUR START WITH STITCHERY? I had purchased the entire series of *The X-Files* for a friend of mine. I found myself spending seven hours a day, stuck to the television, enjoying the shows but doing nothing else. So I thought about how I had always wanted to try my hand at embroidery. It worked out well. It was something I could do while watching *The X-Files*. **HOW DO YOU SELECT YOUR SUBJECT MATTER?** With my embroidery, I want to try and focus more on topics that might not normally be seen in this medium. Topics that I feel should be thought on, but that go contrary to the softer, more homely, simpler feel so often associated with the craft of embroidery.

WILLIAM SCHAFF

THE STAGE NAMES
2007 | 7 x 5 inches (17.8 x 12.7 cm)
Cotton thread, white linen; hand embroidered
Photo by artist

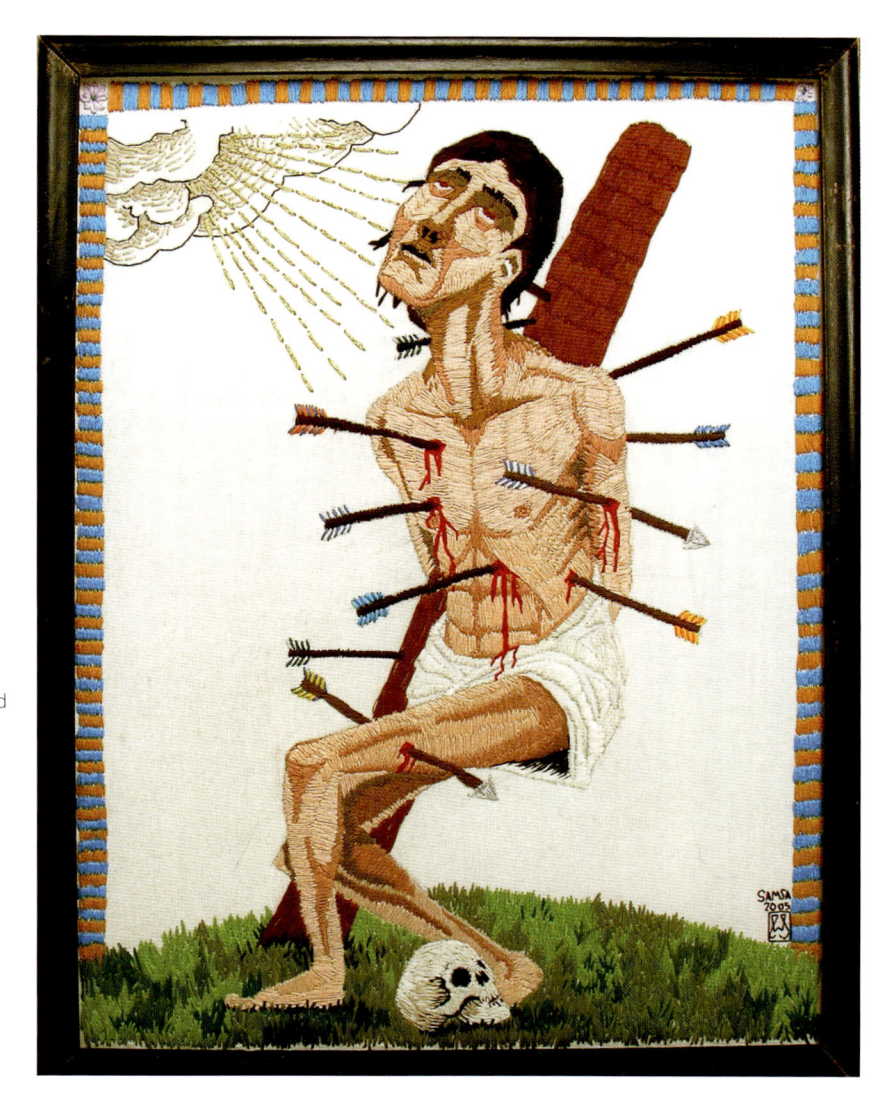

ST. SEBASTIAN

2005 | 24 x 18 inches (61 x 45.7 cm)
Cotton thread, white cotton; hand embroidered
Photo by artist

WILLIAM SCHAFF

AYA KAKEDA
UNITED STATES

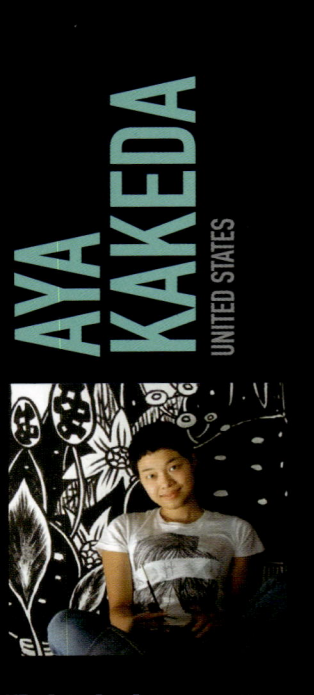

"I think this sentimental and sweet medium works with my dark and scary narratives."

YASHITA TRIBE RITUAL BLANKET
2007 | 12 x 23 inches (30.5 x 58.4 cm)
Threads, felt, fabric; embroidered
Photos by artist

▲ **ACE HOTEL INSTALLATION**
2009 | 60 x 96 inches (152.4 x 243.8 cm)
Threads, felt, fabric; embroidered
Photo by Duc Nicolas

HOW DID YOU END UP IN THIS PARTICULAR MEDIUM? My grandmother on my mother's side was a tea-ceremony teacher, and she wore a kimono all the time. Sometimes the kimono maker would come to our house and open rolls and rolls of beautiful textiles to show her. I loved seeing the artistic patterns and textures of those rolls. My grandmother on my father's side is a great craft maker. She would make dolls, wall decorations, and quilts and send them to us for presents. So I've been fascinated by textiles since an early age. I think this sentimental and sweet medium works with my dark and scary narratives. I love the contrast between the medium and what it really says. **DESCRIBE YOUR**

▲ **STORY OF MY LITTLE BABIES**
2009 | 11 x 16 inches (27.9 x 40.6 cm)
Threads, felt, fabric; dyed, embroidered
Photo by artist

TECHNIQUE AND WORKING PROCESS. When I do my embroidery, I usually do it freehand because I love the childlike, non-profound lines that I get. Sometimes I feel my drawings and paintings are too stiff and controlled, so I'm trying to keep an uncontrolled line quality with my embroidery. But I'm always interested in new techniques; I research when

ADVENTURE OF 3 CHILDREN AND AN EVIL NANNY (CENTER IMAGE)
2004 | 18 x 24 inches (45.7 x 61 cm)
Threads, felt, fabric; embroidered
Photo by artist

I travel or go to museums to look through tapestries, embroideries, and costumes **WHAT INSPIRES YOU AND YOUR WORK?** Everyday silly conversations with friends, films, books, the New York Public Library picture collections, the science page of the *New York Times*. Traveling also always inspires me.

ANDREA VANDER KOOIJ
CANADA

"I usually use vintage or reclaimed materials as a point of departure for my work."

▲ SKELETAL SQUIRREL
2006 | 17½ x 17½ x 1¾ inches (44.5 x 44.5 x 4.4 cm)
Vintage bed sheet; hand embroidered
Photo by Kate Fellerath

HATCHLING
2007 | 12 x 12 x 1¾ inches
(30.5 x 30.5 x 4.4 cm)
Vintage pillowcase;
hand embroidered
Photo by Kate Fellerath

Q&A

HOW DO YOU DESCRIBE YOUR WORK? I usually use vintage or reclaimed materials as a point of departure for my work. I spend a lot of time sourcing and accumulating them, which are integral and enjoyable parts of my process. I also often use found imagery, such as didactic illustrations from old how-to books and discarded notes that I've found on the street. **HOW DID YOU GET YOUR START WITH EMBROIDERY?** My drawings never turned out to look how I wanted them to, but with embroidery I was able to make things that looked like the things I saw in my head. I've been embroidering since I was about 11 years old, but I didn't start incorporating embroidery into my art practice until I was in school.

ANDREA VANDER KOOIJ 133

◆ **SAC NOIR (BLACK BAG)**
2008 | 27 x 23 x 2 inches (68.6 x 58.4 x 5.1 cm)
Cotton, found note; hand embroidered
Translated note reads: "The Cat is in the black bag inside of the garbage can. Please leave the garbage can."
Photos by Kate Fellerath

The work that I did then was received with such a variety of very strong reactions that I knew I was on the right track. **WHAT INSPIRES YOU?** Kids' books, vintage bed sheets, and long drives in the car are always very good for my work. Bad handwriting, accidental beauty—like the shape of paint spills—and vintage magazines are also big favorites. **WHAT PLACE DOES EMBROIDERY HAVE IN THE ART WORLD?** Embroidery work still has a bit of an outsider status in the traditional art world, and while that can sometimes be annoying, it can also be advantageous. I think there are things you can say

🔺 **LUCHADOR**
2007 | 17 x 15½ inches (43.2 x 39.4 cm)
Vintage fabric; appliqué, embroidery
Photo by Kate Fellerath

🔺 **KOI**
2007 | 19 x 12 x 1¾ inches (48.3 x 30.5 x 4.4 cm)
Vintage pillowcase; appliqué, hand embroidered
Photo by Kate Fellerath

more easily with embroidery than with other media, because of the associations that the viewer brings to the work. When you use embroidery in your artwork you are accessing a whole history that is radically different from, say, painting. It also holds some sort of awkward shock value, since it is traditionally considered to be a craft medium. So depending on how you use it, there is the possibility of being subtly subversive with embroidery.

MEAGAN ILEANA
UNITED STATES

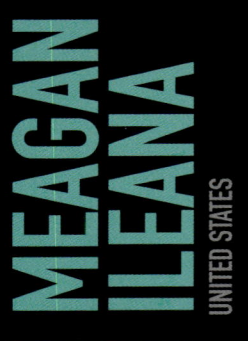

"My work is based on the lines and curves of the female nude form, using embroidery floss on white cotton fabric. Most pieces contain self-portraits of simple and sweet moments of my life."

ROOT DEEP
2008 | 12½ x 6 inches (31.8 x 15.2 cm)
Cotton embroidery floss, cotton, watercolor; hand embroidered
Photo by artist

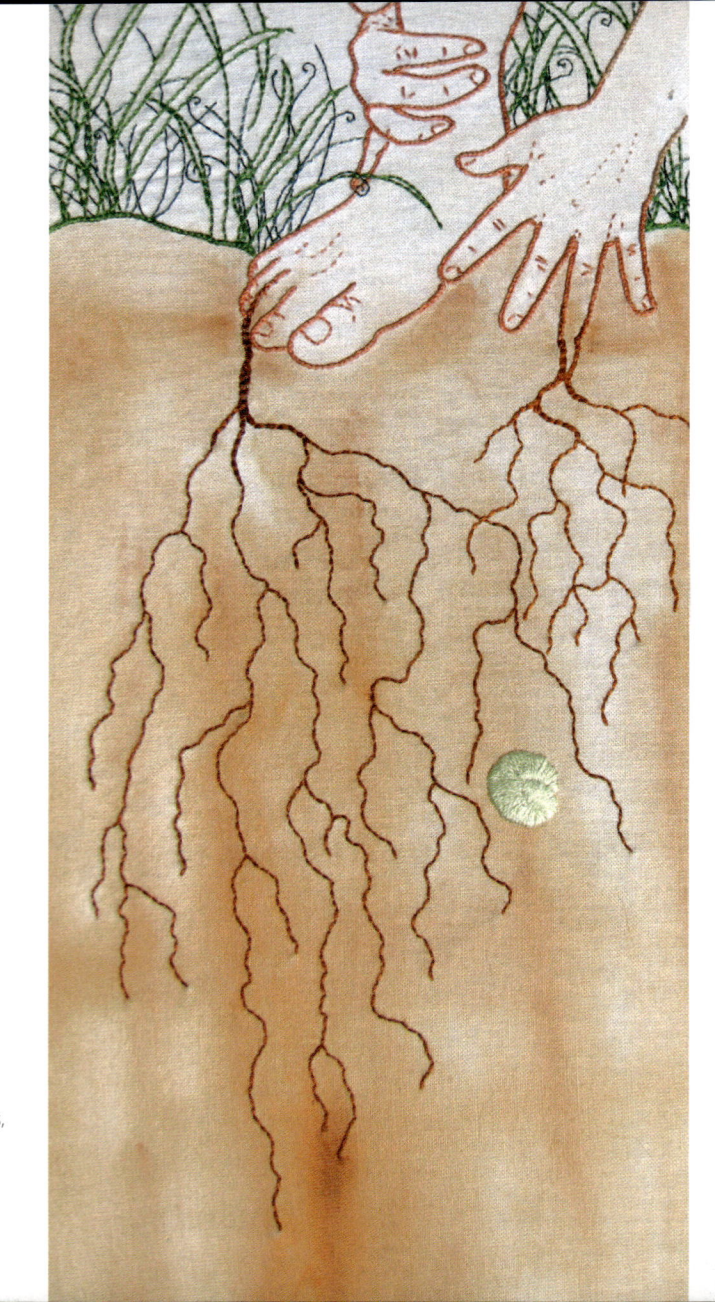

FINGERPRINTS
2009 | 7 x 7½ inches (17.8 x 19.1 cm)
Cotton embroidery floss, cotton; hand embroidered
Photo by artist

Q&A

HOW DID YOU GET YOUR START WITH EMBROIDERY? Following the tradition of the women in my family, I began stitching very early on but only in adulthood did I seriously return to embroidery to discover that it is very versatile. **HOW HAS YOUR SUBJECT MATTER EVOLVED?** In the beginning the pieces were more about the audacity of using embroidery to create images of nudes. As time has progressed the pieces have become more about emotions, and the lens has turned inward to bring out a more honest narrative. **WHAT NEW WORKING PROCESSES HAVE YOU DEVELOPED?** I have begun to open up the process to embrace other media, including photography. This makes the creative process longer and more

MEAGAN ILEANA 137

involved, which I appreciate. I use various transfer methods interspersed with sketching, maintaining a freedom for the image to change as it is created. **WHERE DO YOU FIND YOUR INSPIRATION?** I often draw on the intimate moments of life for inspiration. A private moment between lovers, desire, yearning to return home, the joy of being naked…I also

GRASS BETWEEN MY TOES
2009 | 7½ x 6½ inches (19.1 x 16.5 cm)
Cotton embroidery floss, cotton;
hand embroidered
Photo by artist

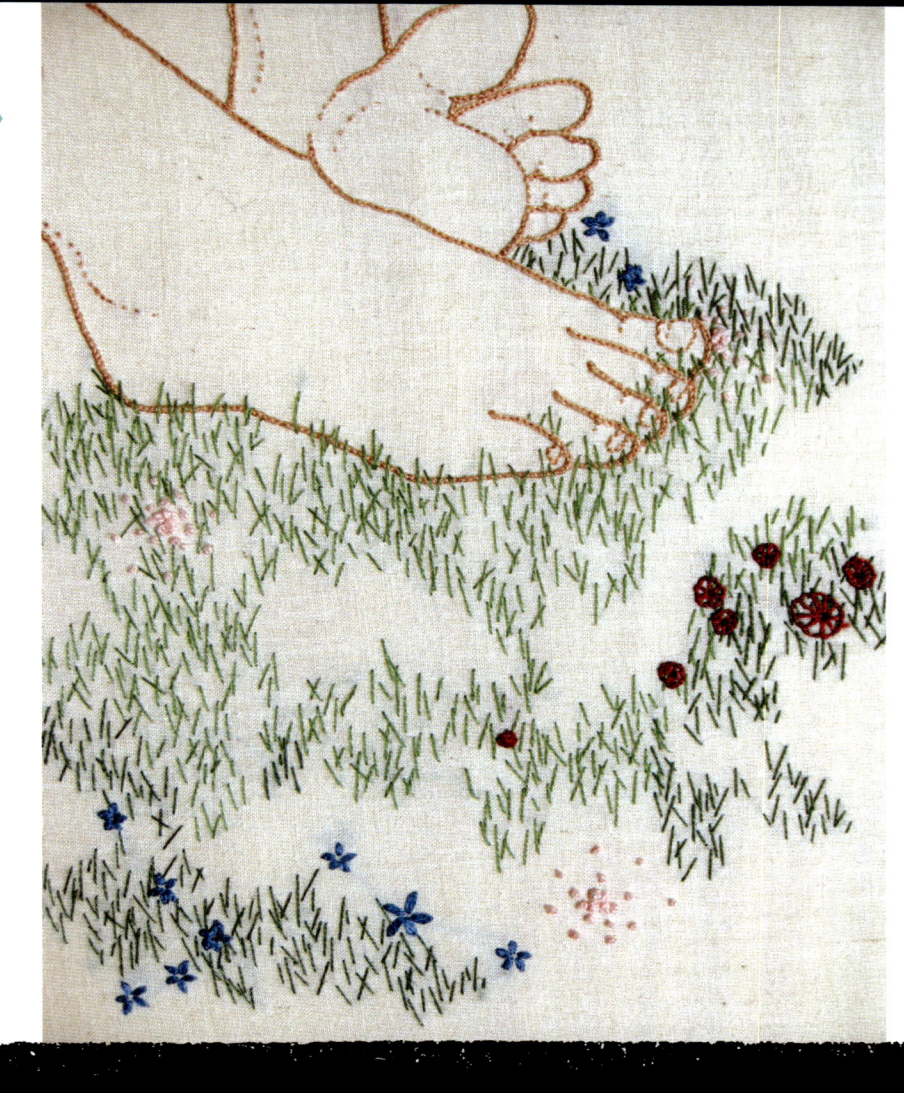

LEFT TO SLEEP
2009 | 7½ x 10¾ inches (19.1 x 27.3 cm)
Cotton embroidery floss, cotton; hand embroidered
Photo by artist

find small living things such as plants and babies to be very inspirational. **HAS YOUR TECHNIQUE CHANGED OVER TIME?** Over time my stitches have become smaller, and the lines that create the images are much smoother. There is more consistency in the quality of the lines and shapes. I am approaching new stitches and techniques with more confidence.

MEAGAN ILEANA

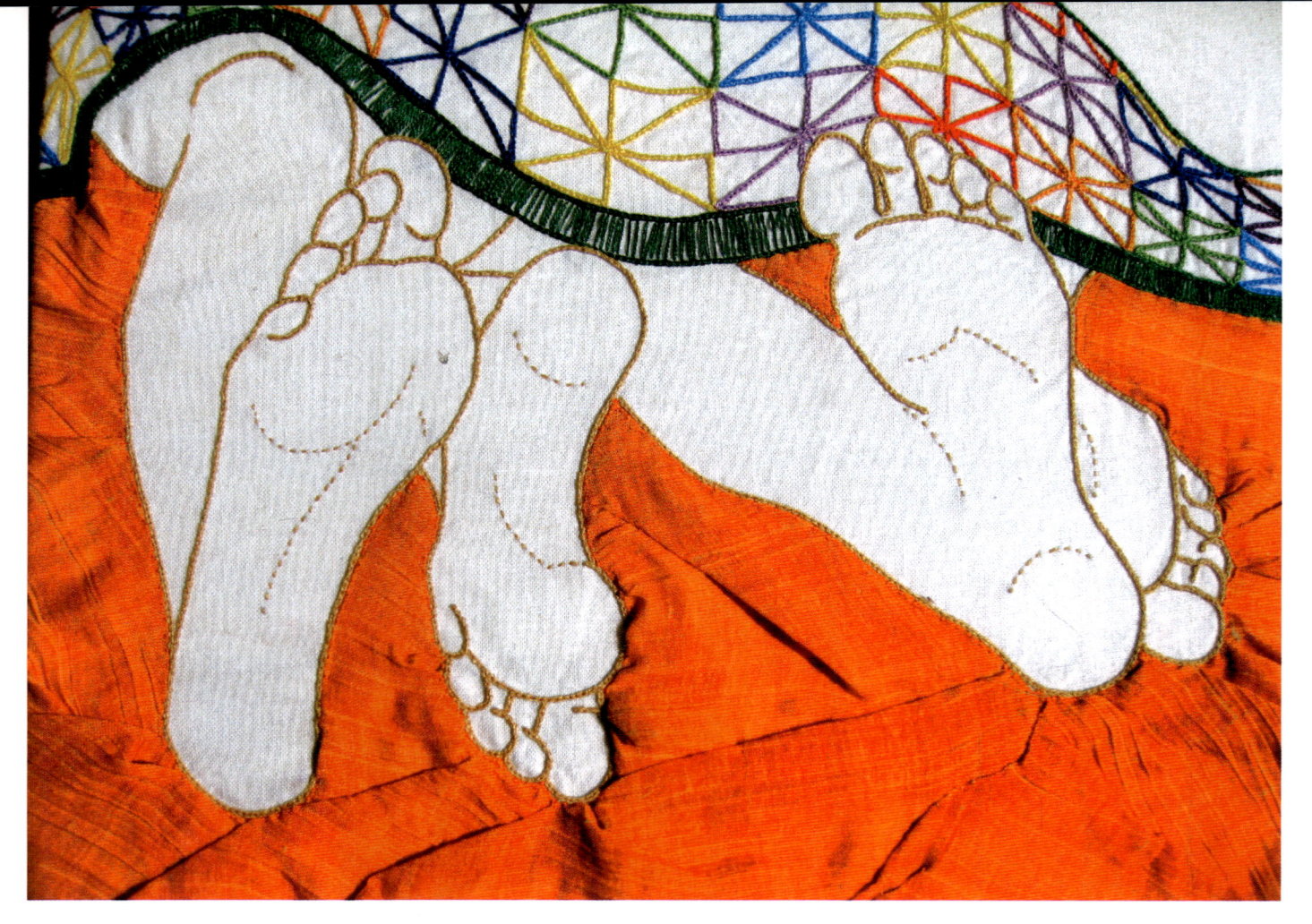

SNUGGLE

2008 | 10 x 10 inches (25.4 x 25.4 cm)
Cotton embroidery floss, cotton;
hand embroidered, appliqué
Photo by artist

DANDELION
2009 | 4¼ x 5¾ inches (10.8 x 14.6 cm)
Cotton embroidery floss, cotton;
hand embroidered
Photo by artist

MEAGAN ILEANA

ANNA TORMA
CANADA

"I produce images and narrative elements that relate to collage, sketching, and drawing while retaining the sensations and implied touch of fiber art."

◀ **FOLKLORE I.**
2009 | 86⅝ x 70⅞ inches (220 x 180 cm)
Linen base, mercerized cotton threads; embroidered
Photos by Istvan Zsako

HAS YOUR TECHNIQUE CHANGED OR DEVELOPED OVER TIME? The technique is subordinate to the content. On collage pieces, I use the stitches to hold together the parts; on others I use the running and satin stitches as a drawing tool, leaving permanent marks on different fabric bases. **HOW HAS YOUR SUBJECT MATTER EVOLVED?** I move between figuration and abstraction, between the decorative and the literal in text, image, and narrative in my pieces. My work also deals with the possible variations of male-female characteristics and the connections they have with each other. **TELL ME ABOUT YOUR LATEST WORK.** In my latest body of work, I used three layers of silk fabrics. The middle layer has bright prints,

METAMORPHOSIS

2008 | 78¾ x 63 inches (200 x 160 cm)
Silk, linen base, found objects, lace appliqué; hand embroidered
Photo by Istvan Zsako

visible through the transparent white silk back and front layer. The front layer is heavily embroidered with silk threads. The interaction between the dense stitches and the fine silk layers creates a relief-like surface that gives the work an extra dimension. **HOW DID YOU END UP IN THIS PARTICULAR MEDIUM?** I had small children and embroidery was

TRANSVERBAL I.
2010 | 57 1/16 x 51 15/16 inches
(145 x 132 cm)
Three layers of fine silk, silk threads;
hand embroidered
Photo by Istvan Zsako

TRANSVERBAL V.
2010 | 57 1/16 x 51 15/16 inches
(145 x 132 cm)
Three layers of fine silk, silk threads; hand embroidered
Photo by Istvan Zsako

the only possible choice to practice visual art. **WHAT INSPIRES YOU THESE DAYS?** My works are influenced by Visionary and Outsider art. Its expressive directness and ability to communicate emotions to a wide range of viewers are important aspects of my creative choices.

DONNA SHARRETT

UNITED STATES

"I make objects to serve as placeholders of memory using symbolically significant materials."

146

◀ WILD HORSES

2007 | 32 x 32 inches (81.3 x 81.3 cm)
Rose petals, handmade rose beads, synthetic hair, guitar-string ball-ends, pennies, bone beads, garnets, dirt, rings, synthetic pearls, cotton shirting, hand-embroidered damask linen, blue jeans, cookie cutters, and thread; crochet, embroidery, needlelace
Photos by Margaret Fox

Q&A

HOW DO YOU DESCRIBE YOUR WORK? I make objects to serve as placeholders of memory using symbolically significant materials, many of which are donated, including guitar, violin, and harp strings; rose petals; antique damask linens; and clothing. The circular forms and compositions reflect the seamless continuum of ritual that binds the past to the present, and the present to the future. Mirroring the Buddhist mandala form, the circular shape enveloped by the square background characterizes the infinite within the finite. The geometric schemes of Gothic cathedral rose

SILENCE

2007-2009 | 24 x 24 inches (61 x 61 cm)
Rose petals, synthetic hair, guitar-string ball-ends, harp-string ball-ends, blue jeans, hand-embroidered damask linen, silk neckties and fabric, rings, garnets, bone beads, synthetic pearls, and thread; crochet, embroidery, needlelace
Photos by Margaret Fox

windows and the numeric configurations of religious prayer beads inform the mathematical arrangements of the work. I also use rings, bone beads, dirt, and handmade rose beads inspired by a 13th-century recipe for rosary beads. Guitar-string ball ends are used as a dedication to my brother, Scot Sharrett, as are the song titles chosen

LONG BLACK VEIL

2003-2008 | 26 x 26 inches (66 x 66 cm)
Rose petals, handmade rose beads, synthetic hair, guitar-string ball-ends, pennies, blue jeans, cotton shirting, rings, bone beads and buttons, garnets, synthetic pearls, and thread; crochet, embroidery, needlelace
Photos by Margaret Fox

to name the works. **HOW HAVE YOUR TECHNIQUE AND SUBJECT MATTER EVOLVED?** Research informs my work and leads to new techniques, working processes, and expanded nuances within my subject matter. **WHERE DO YOU DRAW INSPIRATION?** Beauty in nature and art.

LOUISE RILEY
UNITED KINGDOM

"My work explores the affair between nature and society. Are they symbiotic or opposing forces and which is the bigger beast?"

150

FILM STILL
2008 | 39⅜ x 39⅜ x 11¹³⁄₁₆ inches
(100 x 100 x 30 cm)
Foam, mattress skin, thread
Photo by artist

JOINED AT THE HIP AND BENT OVER BACKWARDS
2008 | 39⅜ x 78¾ x 39⅜ inches (1 x 2 x 1 m)
Floorboards, mattress skin, foam, thread and silk wool
Photo by artist

Q&A

HOW DO YOU DESCRIBE YOUR WORK? My work explores the affair between nature and society. Are they symbiotic or opposing forces and which is the bigger beast? I look at how these phenomena steer relationships, the force of procreation, and life outcomes. I have looked to biology and chemistry, literally and metaphorically; I have looked to textiles, with their array of DNA-like constructions to find the solutions, the logic in this chaos. Discarded mattresses form the backbone of the works, for their inbuilt personal history—both corporeal and spiritual—to create a domestic wonderland of human experience. **HOW HAS YOUR TECHNIQUE AND WORKING PROCESS DEVELOPED?** They are developing all

LOUISE RILEY

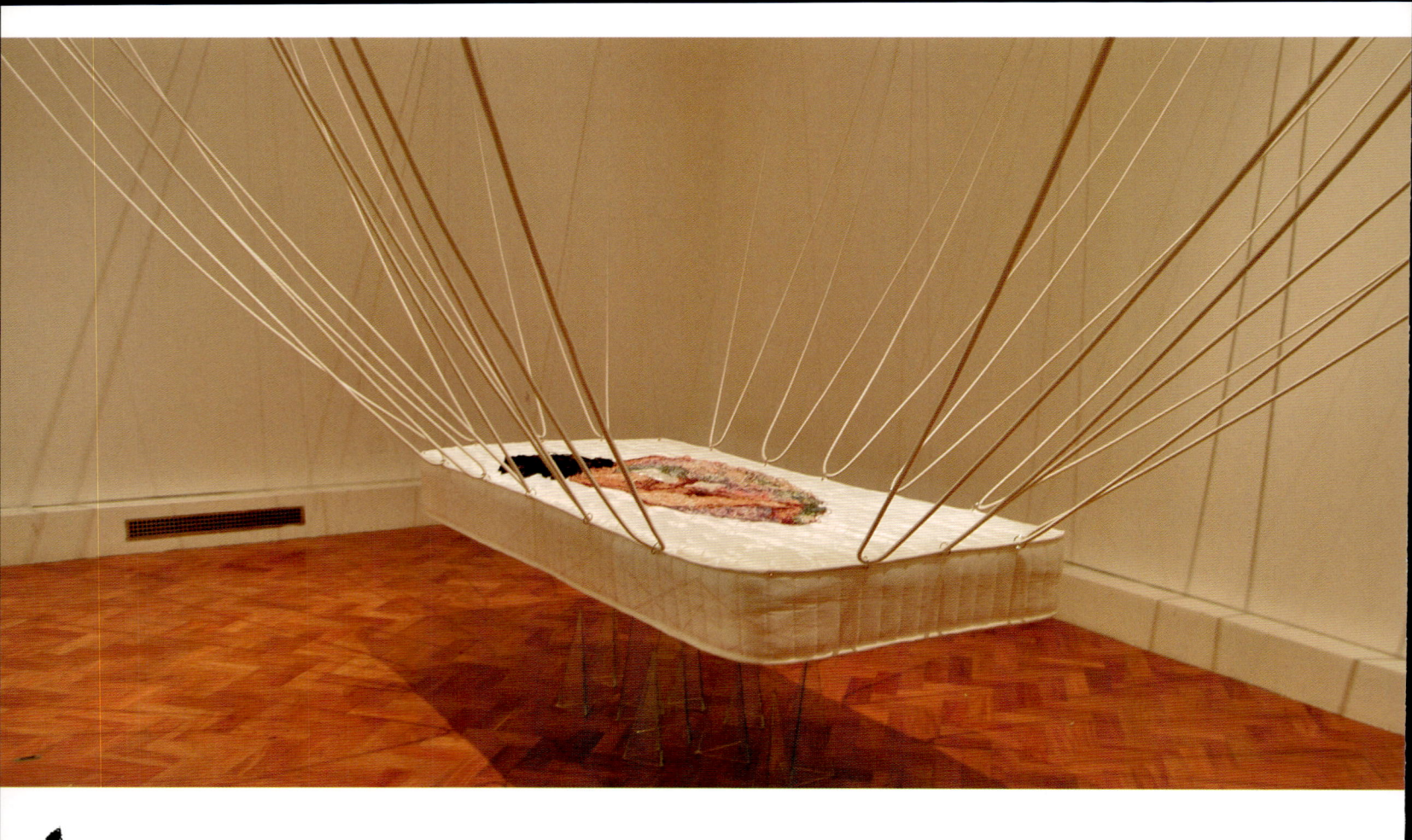

the time. I like to have a technical adventure with every batch of work, so I rarely have a chance to get cocky. So it is always a challenge; this keeps it honest. With the new series, for instance, I got such a bad neck ache from working on the big mattresses on the floor that I decided that my next work would be all done standing up and waving my

MOTHER OF PEARL
2010 | 137¹³⁄₁₆ x 196⅞ x 118⅛ inches
(3.5 x 5 x 3 m)
Glass, mattress, thread and wool, bungee cord,
key rings, eyelets, silk velvet
Photo by artist

LIGHT PERSPECTIVE
2010 | 118⅛ x 78¾ x 39⅜ inches (3 x 2 x1 m)
Foam, mattress skins, carpet scraps, thread
Photo by artist

arms around. It is not always the art that dictates the process; life gets involved, too. **WHAT INSPIRES YOU THESE DAYS?** At the moment I am thinking about varying perceptions of reality, weather patterns, virtual landscapes made from unexpected sources, and creating the equivalent of rose-tinted glasses in a large form.

LOUISE RILEY

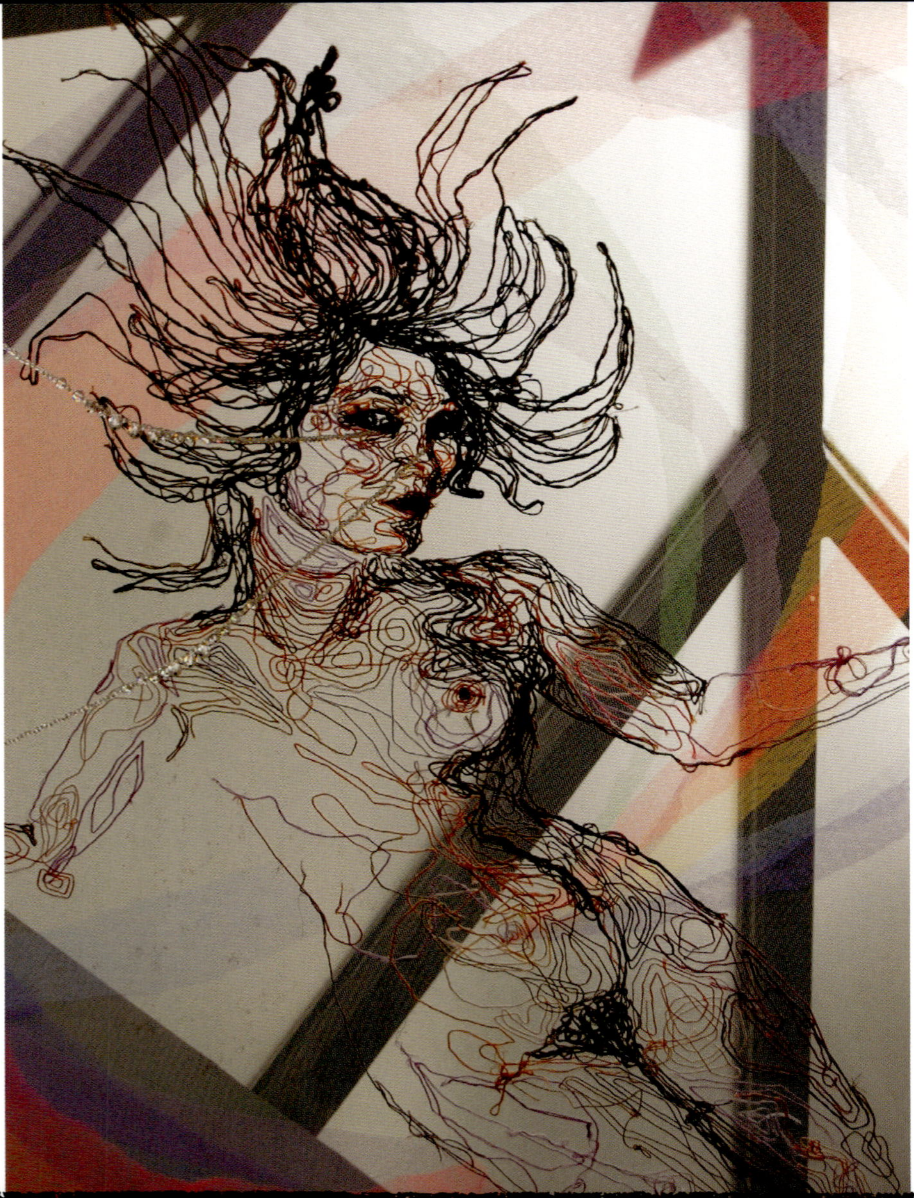

◀ **CORDELIA: "THE SOUL WOULD HAVE NO RAINBOW IF THE EYE HAD NO TEARS" — NATIVE AMERICAN PROVERB**
2010 | 118⅛ x 78¾ x 39⅜ inches (3 x 2 x 1 m)
Net, bicycle wheels, jewels, crystals, necklaces, magnets, thread
Photos by artist

ROBERT FORMAN
UNITED STATES

"I glue threads of cotton, linen, silk, and rayon to clayboard."

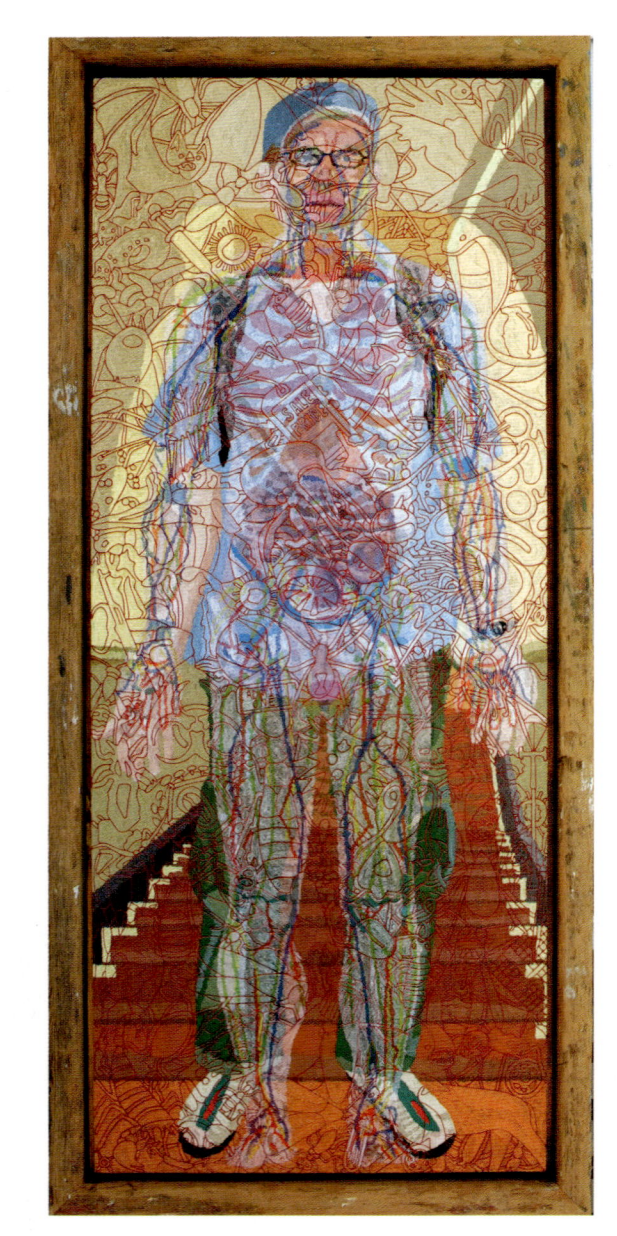

◀ INFESTATION
2010 | 45 x 18 inches (114.3 x 45.7 cm)
Thread, board; glued
Photos by Robin Schwartz

156

▲ FRAME SHOP
2003 | 24 x 36 inches
(61 x 91.4 cm)
Thread, board; glued
Photo by Jeff Goldman

HOW DID YOU END UP IN THIS PARTICULAR MEDIUM? For 40 years I've been asked this question, but I still do not have a simple answer. I was making paintings and collages while in high school. At some point, I glued some of my mother's embroidery thread to a collage and ended up covering most of the picture with it. I had begun drawing at the same time, and the line of the thread and the line of the pencil reinforced each other. When I went to art school (The Cooper Union), I spent the first semester painting and drawing. My professors commented that I drew well but painted like I'd never held a brush before. When a professor (Jack Whitten) asked what we did during Christmas vacation,

ROBERT FORMAN 157

DRIVING
2005 | 16 x 56 inches (40.6 x 142.2 cm)
Thread, board; glued
Photo by Jeff Goldman

I mentioned my thread painting. I was told to bring one in and was encouraged to continue and that it would be considered painting. I've been at it ever since. **HAVE YOU DEVELOPED ANY NEW WORKING PROCESSES?** The basic process has not changed since I began gluing thread in 1969. **HOW MUCH PLANNING DOES IT TAKE TO DO PAINTED THREAD WORK?** I spend a

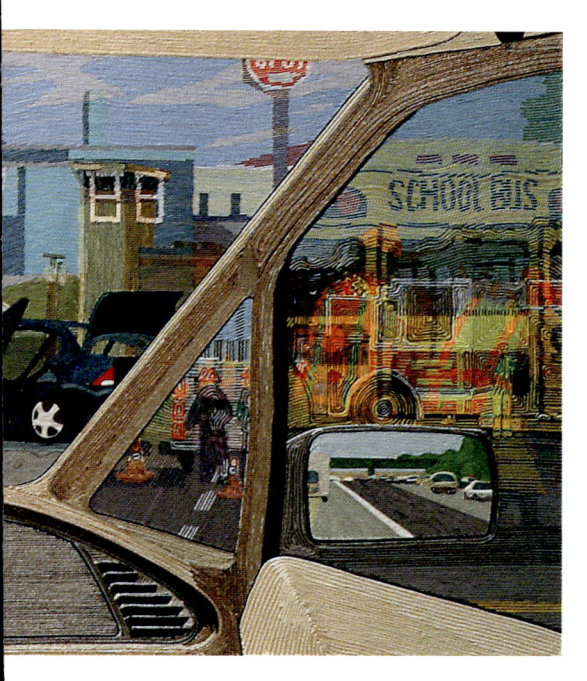

▲ **SPANISH LESSONS**
2003 | 24 x 36 inches (61 x 91.4 cm)
Thread, board; glued
Photo by Jeff Goldman

lot of time planning a new work. After settling on a concept and a size, I draw detailed full-size cartoons from which I base the final picture. I've learned that the more preliminary work I do, the more attention I can spend on developing the actual piece. **WHERE DO YOU FIND INSPIRATION?** I try to keep myself open to serendipitous inspiration.

ROBERT FORMAN 159

DAD
2009 | 15 x 36 inches (38.1 x 91.4 cm)
Thread, board; glued
Photo by Robin Schwartz

DOG WALKING
2007 | 20 x 30 inches
(50.8 x 76.2 cm)
Thread, board; glued
Photo by Jeff Goldman

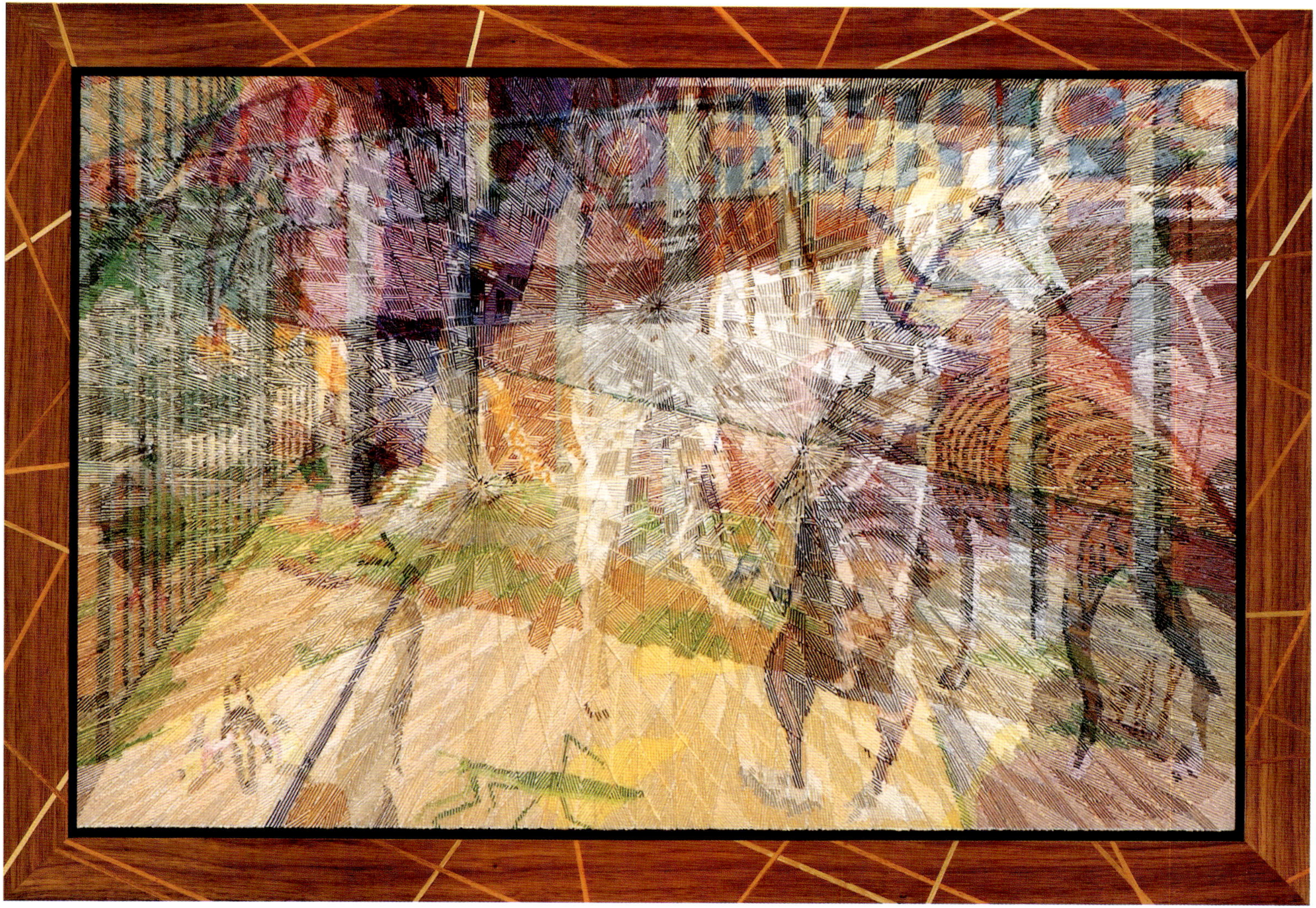

JIMMY MCBRIDE
UNITED STATES

"I work for an intergalactic shipping company, and I've got a lot of time on my hands. The views out my window provide amazing inspiration for the quilts that I make."

THE PILLARS OF CREATION
1523 P.C. | 81 x 73 inches (205.7 x 185.4 cm)
Clothes from an outpost in the Outer Rim, thread from a daikon farmer; hand made and hand quilted
Photos by artist

Q&A

HOW DID YOU GET YOUR START IN QUILTING? I downloaded a grandma program, and she's teaching me how to quilt. There are giant lags between land leave, and quilting seemed to be a great way to pass the time. **HAVE YOU DEVELOPED ANY NEW WORKING PROCESSES?** Most of grandma's programs are for basic patterns: triangles, squares, etc. I've really had to improvise to get the sweeping views of the universe to translate to quilts. All of the quilts are pieced together, so I've gotten really good at curves, tight spots, and miniature pieces. **HOW MUCH PLANNING DOES IT TAKE TO DO YOUR QUILTS?**

◀ **NGC2264 (THE CONE NEBULA)**
1523 P.C. | 52 x 46 inches (132.1 x 116.8 cm)
Fabric from a trading post on a far moon, thread from a witch; hand made and hand quilted
Photos by artist

To make the pattern takes a couple of days, and then trying to piece together enough scrap fabric and thread can take a while. But, once that's all assembled, it takes between one to three months to complete one, depending on whether I'm machine or hand quilting it. **WHERE DO YOU FIND INSPIRATION FOR YOUR WORK?** My route isn't horribly consistent,

AMBUSH IN QUADRANT 4 ON THE FAR SIDE OF THE PLEIADES
1524 P.C. | 75 x 88 inches (190.5 x 223.5 cm)
Fabric from three colonies and one space station, thread from a trading market on a far moon and a nice old lady; hand made and machine quilted
Photo by artist

so I constantly get to see new things and meet new people and cultures. Also, I pick up new techniques and materials whenever I meet new colonists or fellow travelers.

R136 IN 30 DORADUS

1524 P.C. | 78 x 77 inches (198.1 x 195.6 cm)
Fabric and thread from five colonies, two space ports, and the Oracle on Caster's moon; hand made and machine quilted
Photo by artist

M64 (THE BLACK EYE GALAXY)

1522 P.C. | 60 x 45 inches (152.4 x 114.3 cm)
Clothing salvaged from a deserted colony; hand made and hand quilted
Photos by artist

JIMMY MCBRIDE 167

THE ARTISTS / INDEX

RAQUEL J. ALVES (PAGE 40)
Raquel Alves has made many websites and other designs, and frequently experiments with analog photography. Starting in 2008, Alves began working with collage, and has found it is the medium that best allows her to mix textures, colors, photographs, threads, textiles, drawings, and more in order to achieve a natural, hand-crafted product. She enjoys using her own hands to manipulate and toy with actual things, which is why she is drawn to analog photography and collage.

Photo on page 40 by the artist.

raquel-j-alves.blogspot.com

GILLIAN BATES (PAGE 90)
Gillian Bates produces contemporary textile art in the form of wall-hung canvases. All of her handmade canvases are entirely unique and created using reclaimed and vintage fabrics. Her obsession for all things textile led her to successfully gain a BA (with Honors) in Textile and Surface Design in 2007. She is now very happy to indulge her passion working as a full-time artist, creating contemporary textile art from her studio based in the elegant Sussex seaside town of Eastbourne, England.

www.gillianbates.co.uk

JENNIFER BOE (PAGE 84)
Jennifer Boe, originally of Northern Indiana, received her B.F.A. in Painting and Creative Writing in 2001 from the Kansas City Art Institute. She made the transition to embroidery a year later. Her work is a combination of the aesthetic and artistic philosophy gained as a writer and painter, as well as the crafts of her childhood. Boe lives and works in Kansas City, Missouri, with her husband and studio-mate, Andy Maugh. Her work has been exhibited nationally and internationally including: Late Show, Kansas City; Greenlease, Kansas City; Ellipse Arts Center, Virginia; and Triennale Museum, Milan.

Photo on page 84 by M. Andy Maugh.

www.boemaugh.com

DIEM CHAU (PAGE 54)
Diem Chau and her family came to America as refugees from Vietnam in 1986. Chau is a BFA graduate from Cornish College of the Arts. Her work has been featured in *Harpers*, *Fiberarts*, *ReadyMade*, and *American Craft Magazine*. Chau combines common mediums and common means to create delicate vignettes of fleeting memory, gesture, and form. The resulting work combines egalitarian sensibility and minimalist restraint. Her work touches on the value of Storytelling, Myths, and their ability to connect us to each other through cultural and humanistic similarities. Chau's current work drifts into the periphery narrative, moments forgotten and faded, or too brief to retain.

Photo on page 54 by the artist.

www.diemchau.com

ORLY COGAN (PAGE 58)
Orly Cogan was educated at The Cooper Union in New York and The Maryland Institute College of Art. She has had solo exhibitions at galleries in Chicago, Los Angeles, San Francisco, and Kansas City and has participated in many group shows in New York galleries. Cogan has participated in several museum exhibitions and her work has been published in several museum catalogs and books. She has been reviewed in the *New York Times*, the *Chicago Sun Times*, *The American Art Collector*, and *Art Forum* among others.

Photo on page 58 by OC Studio.

www.orlycogan.com

PETER CRAWLEY (PAGE 74)

Peter Crawley is a trained and practicing Product Designer, and is Senior Designer at a small London-based product design consultancy. His design work ranges from domestic house wares to street furniture and public transport infrastructure. Crawley's stitched illustrations have been heavily influenced by his keen and constantly developing interest in product design, geometry, architecture and public structures. His illustrations continue to develop, regularly including new subject areas, styles, techniques, and materials. Crawley has worked on various self-initiated and commissioned illustrations.

Photo on page 74 by the artist.

www.petercrawley.co.uk

MARLOES DUYKER (PAGE 108)

Marloes Duyker's works are made up of structures and details, purity, the beauty of imperfection, and spontaneity. Her work is created by the sewing machine to produce textile pieces that balance between figurative and abstract worlds—a delicate game of structures and fragile stitching. Duyker (Naked Design) designs remarkable concepts and 2D and 3D images for editorial purposes, display windows, stands, fashion, jewelry, and furniture. As an artist, Duyker gratefully uses the contrast between the technique and subjects like suicide, the depression, and the loss of identity. This is varied by light-hearted and spontaneous images of colorful birds, styled man-figures, and poetic portraits.

Photo on page 108 by Anneke Jakobs.

www.nakeddesign.nl

EMILY EIBEL (PAGE 118)

Emily L. Eibel is an illustrator and fine artist who wants a cabin in the woods, but for now she is living and working in Brooklyn, New York. In 2004, she graduated from Pratt Institute. Since then she has illustrated for such publications as *The New Yorker*, the *New York Times*, *McSweeney's*, and *Wired Magazine*. Her stitched work has been shown in galleries throughout the US and internationally. See more of her work online at www.emilyeibel.com and www.tombyillustration.com.

Photo on page 118 by Jashar Awan.

www.emilyeibel.com

ROBERT FORMAN (PAGE 156)

Robert Forman received a BFA in painting in 1975 at The Cooper Union School of Art. He has received Artist Fellowships from the National Endowment for the Arts, The Adolph and Esther Gottlieb Foundation, The New Jersey State Council on the Arts, and the Ludwig Vogelstein Foundation. In 1992 Forman traveled to Mexico as a Fulbright Fellow to meet and talk shop with fellow yarn painters among the Huichol, an indigenous people working in a similar medium. Forman is represented by Francis M. Naumann Fine Art in New York City.

Photo on page 156 by Robin Schwartz.

www.glueyarn.com

LUKE HAYNES (PAGE 68)

Luke Haynes creates scenes, images, portraits and environments out of fabric and thread. Drawing from a tradition of meditative American portraiture, with influences ranging from Chuck Close to Kehinde Wiley, Haynes depicts the images with which we find comfort. His pieces are constructed within the traditional quilting process: layering cloth pieces, inscribed by thread. With roots in the American South, and an architectural

THE ARTISTS / INDEX

education at Cooper Union, his work lies within the juncture between form and function, art and craft, quilt tradition and contemporary design culture.

Photo on page 68 by David Papas.

www.lukehaynes.com

BASCOM HOGUE (PAGE 48)

Bascom Hogue is a self-taught artist, a native Kansan, and a Mennonite. He grew up on his grandfather's farm and salvage yard, but his asthma often kept him indoors. In order to help pass the time, two of his mother's tailor friends taught him to sew clothes and the Mennonite women taught him to sew other textiles. These early life craft skills enabled hiimto forge ahead and become a self-taught artist. Hogue is also an ordained preacher and social worker.

Photo on page 48 by Mrs. Hogue.

cottonwooddiner.blogspot.com

MEAGAN ILEANA (PAGE 136)

Meagan Ileana began stitching while living in the Himalayas with her family at the age of three and has been lucky enough to continue to travel extensively around the world—including more than four years in India. Most recently she returned to India to gather inspiration and explore Indian handmade textiles and embroidery. She has made a home in the beautiful hills of Southern Indiana in a wonderful community where she is learning the delights of organic gardening and urban homesteading. Ileana feels that art is the only way for her to express her appreciation of life's beauty.

Photo on page 136 by the artist.

www.meaganileana.com

SEVERIJA INČIRAUSKAITÉ-KRIAUNEVIČIENÉ (PAGE 16)

Severija Inčirauskaité-Kriaunevičiené has been, perhaps, always "in art." She grew up in a family of artists and almost inside the Telšiai Applied Arts Polytechnic (now a part of the Applied Arts Faculty of the Vilnius Academy of Fine Arts) where her parents had been teaching. She has known the specific characteristics of metal since childhood—its solidity, heaviness, flexibility, and fragility—and also the tangled nature of threads and the softness of textiles. Unsurprisingly, she has been drawing from the arsenal of both areas in her art, using everythin they can offer.

Photo on page 16 by Tomas Kriaunevići

www.severija.lt

ROSIE JAMES (PAGE 34)

Rosie James was born in England and brought up in Liverpool. She worked fo some years as a Radiographer before her passion for fabric got the better of her. Rosie studied Printed Textiles at UCA Farnham and then received a MA i Fine Art Textiles at Goldsmiths College in London. Since then she has immerse herself in her textiles life—creating, exhibiting, and teaching to such an ext that she has never felt the need to retu to Radiography. She currently lives in semi-rural Kent, where she is learning t play the piano accordion, which is scari the local cats.

Photo on page 34 by the artist.

www.axisweb.org/artist/rosiejames

CÉCILE JARSAILLON (PAGE 114)

Cécile Jarsaillon has been a part of the French punk rock underground scene since 1994. She is a singer, songwriter, guitarist, and experimental theatre actress who tours the country with shows and concerts. For the past ten years, she has been a completely self-taught painter, sculptor, and embroiderer. This dual identity feeds her works, and the duality of agitation and peace allows her to quietly tackle shocking issues.

peinturescecilejarsaillon.blogspot.com

AYA KAKEDA (PAGE 128)

Aya Kakeda has ever-changing monthly obsessions; now it's 14th Century tapestry and naturalist architecture. She also elaborates lots of theories about lots of things. When she doesn't indulge in her obsessions, she sews and draws, creating her own whimsical narratives.

Photo on page 128 by the artist.

www.ayakakeda.com

ANDREA VANDER KOOIJ (PAGE 132)

Andrea Vander Kooij is a Canadian artist who holds an MFA degree, with a concentration in Fibres, from Concordia University. Her practice incorporates traditional craft-based mediums such as knitting, crochet, and embroidery, as well as elements of performance. Her internationally exhibited work addresses gender issues and the body, and challenges the relative valuations of art, craft, and labor. She enjoys working with reclaimed material as well as food. In 2006 she received the Lilianne Elliot Award for Excellence in Fibers. She currently lives in Ontario, Canada with her husband and young son.

Photo on page 132 by Alan Groombridge.

www.andreavanderkooij.com

JOETTA MAUE (PAGE 28)

Joetta Maue is a full-time artist that primarily uses photography and fibers. Her most recent work is a series of embroideries and images exploring intimacy. Joetta received her BFA from Ohio State University and her MFA from the University of Massachusetts. Her work has been shown extensively throughout galleries and museums worldwide. Joetta authors the art and craft blog Little Yellowbird and regularly contributes articles to the online journals Hello Craft and Mr. X Stitch. She was featured in the book Indie Craft (2010). Joetta currently lives and works in Brooklyn, NY, with her husband, son, two cats, and a goldfish. She teaches embroidery and creative arts workshops throughout New York.

Photo on page 28 by the artist.

www.joettamaue.com

JIMMY MCBRIDE (PAGE 162)

Jimmy McBride says, "They say in space, 'no one can hear you scream.' Well, they can't hear the low drone of the internal power generators kick on again when you're halfway to nowhere. I can. I work for a shipping company called Intergalactic Transport. I travel back and forth from rock to rock carrying those two all-important gems: salt and vinegar. There's a lot of time to kill up here so I downloaded a grandma program and she's been teaching me how to quilt. There's not much up here, so I just stare out the window until something catches my eye."

www.jimmymcbride.com

CHARLENE MULLEN (PAGE 102)

Charlene Mullen received an education in textiles and illustration before working in the fashion industry producing print

THE ARTISTS / INDEX

and embroidery designs for fashion labels such as Calvin Klein, Givenchy, and Donna Karan. In 2007, Mullen produced a range of cushions for the launch of Matthew Hilton's range of furniture at 100% Design, where he won "Best Newcomer." This lead Mullen to launch her own range of interior accessories at 100% Design in 2008, where she made the "Best Newcomer" shortlist. Since then she has built the range—exhibiting with the Craft Council at the New York Gift Show in 2010—and her work is stocked in luxury stores across the world, such as Liberty, Le Bon Marche, and Lane Crawford. In addition she has worked on commissions for interior design projects and has signed a license deal with De La Espada, who will launch an exclusive range of her work.

Photo on page 102 by Rachel Smith.

www.charlenemullen.com

PENNY NICKELS (PAGE 44)

Wells Tuthill is an artist who works and writes under the name Penny Nickels. Although her background is in printmaking, she traded her gouges for sewing needles and it changed her life forever. Her husband, Johnny Murder, started the Manbroidery group and together they have been described as "The Bonnie and Clyde of Contemporary Embroidery." They live in an art cave in the Pacific Northwest where she also spins, knits, and weaves.

Photo on page 44 by the artist.

www.donkeywolf.blogspot.com

CLYDE OLLIVER (PAGE 22)

Clyde Oliver began stitching from a very early age and likes to think of embroidery as an approach to making art rather than as any specific technique or material. In recent years he's been stitching, carving, and embroidering slate in various ways; exhibiting his work nationally and internationally; and giving occasional lectures and workshops. He currently lives in the English Lake District, where the glorious countryside affords both raw materials and inspiration.

Photo on page 22 by Lucy Barden.

www.clydeolliver.com

JENNIFER L. PORTER (PAGE 96)

Jennifer L. Porter was born in Fontana, CA, in 1971. In 1997 Jennifer received a Bachelors of Fine Art from the Art Institute of Chicago, followed by a MFA from California Institute of the Arts in 2005, where she studied film and photography with a focus in video art. Jennifer first learned embroidery from her grandmother at the age of nine and then rediscovered it again in 2009 at Reform School/Home Ec. in Silver Lake, CA. She furthered her education at the Royal School of Needlework at Hampton Court Palace outside of London in 2010, where she studied Goldwork. Jennifer currently lives in southern California with her cat, Winifred, and teaches at Chaffey College in the Inland Empire

Photo on page 96 by the artist.

www.porterness.net

LOUISE RILEY (PAGE 150)

Louise Riley lives, breathes, and works in Hackney. She spends her time hoovering in her daughter and other loved ones and then crawls into her cave to exorcise new work. She is inspired through conversation and just the surreal qualities of life: For instance isn't it so weird that buildings are geometric and then there is us wobbling down the road all fleshy and pretty much a bunch of walking meat? Such contrasts blow her mind, to the point of wild inspiration and vertigo/nausea mixed together. An avid biography reader, she is fascinated by peoples' thorny path, that mystifying drive to survive. Her work is presented in diagrams of domestic wonderlands.

Photo on page 150 by Cordelia Weston.

www.louiseriley.co.uk

ALICIA ROSS (PAGE 62)

Alicia Ross's work over the last decade has evolved to encompass various facets of female identity using photography, fiber, video, and installations. Raised in a suburb of Cleveland, Ohio, Ross received her MFA from Rochester Institute of Technology. She now splits her time between Ohio and Texas. Ross's solo exhibition, Sacred_Profane, debuted at Black and White Gallery in Chelsea, New York in 2008, receiving a Critics' Pick from New York Magazine. Ross's work has been published in Flash Art Magazine (International Edition), Saatchi Online, and the Village Voice. Her work continues to appear at art fairs including Art Miami and Pulse New York. Most recently, an interview with Ross was featured on the blog of the PBS documentary series Art21.

Photo on page 62 by the artist.

www.aliciaross.com

WILLIAM SCHAFF (PAGE 124)

William Schaff is a wreck. His most recent job with regular pay involved punching people in the head and hoping they didn't punch him back. That said, he manages to create lots of artwork for different folks. From the likes of fine authors, to such notable independent musicians as Okkervil River, Godspeed You! Black Emperor, and many more. This boy has chops! Chops and debt! Working hard at avoiding debt collectors and making as much art as possible before they catch up with him, this fine artist is just trying to keep his lights on, his car insured, and his mortgage paid. Well, one out of three ain't bad.

Photo on page 124 by the artist.

www.williamschaff.com

TILLEKE SCHWARZ (PAGE 78)

Tilleke Schwarz lives with her husband and cat near Delft in The Netherlands. She was trained at high school and art colleges in The Netherlands and lived for one year near San Francisco as an exchange student. Her sense of humor is typical for her Jewish background: a mixture of a laugh and a tear. Tilleke exhibits all over the world in major galleries and museums. Her work has been published in many magazines and books. She is a freelance lecturer and teacher.

Photo on page 78 by Menno Aarnout.

www.tillekeschwarz.com

DONNA SHARRETT (PAGE 146)

Donna Sharrett is a recipient of several artist's residencies and grants. Her work has been widely exhibited, including a solo exhibition at the Everson Museum in Syracuse, New York. Articles about her work have appeared in the *New York Times*, *Art & Antiques*, *Fiberarts*, *Sculpture Magazine*, *Surface Design*, and the *Frankfurter Allgemeine Zeitung* (Germany). Her work is held in numerous private and public collections including the Museum of Arts & Design in New York City. She holds a degree from the School of Visual Arts in New York City and is represented by Pavel Zoubok Gallery (New York).

Photo on page 146 by Margaret Fox.

www.donnasharrett.com

ANNA TORMA (PAGE 142)

Anna Torma was born in Hungary and received a degree in Textiles from the Hungarian University of Applied Arts. She immigrated to Canada in 1988 and now

173

THE ARTISTS / INDEX

lives in Baie Verte, New Brunswick. She has exhibited her work internationally, including the following public collections: Ministry of Culture, Hungary; Foreign Affairs, Canada; New Brunswick Art Bank; Arkansas Art Center; and Mint Museum of Craft and Design, North Carolina. Her awards include: Strathbutler Award, 2008; City of Tournai Prize, 2008; UNESCO Aschberg Foundation's bursary, 2005; and Chalmers Visual Art Fellowship, 2002.

Photo on page 142 by Nora Herting.

www.annatorma.com

CAYCE ZAVAGLIA (PAGE 10)

Cayce Zavaglia is a painter/embroidery artist working and living in St. Louis, Missouri. She holds a Bachelor of Arts degree from Wheaton College and a Master of Fine Arts Degree in Painting from Washington University. Her embroidered portraits have been included in various portrait shows in galleries and museums and exhibited at PULSE New York, PULSE Miami, and ART MIAMI. Her work has been featured in two editions of New American Paintings and was purchased by the West Collection of Oaks, Pennsylvania. She is currently represented by Lyons Wier Gallery in New York.

Photo on page 10 by the artist.

www.caycezavaglia.com

ACKNOWLEDGMENTS

To all the artists for their creativity and inspiration.
To Amanda and the team at Lark for making this happen.
To Mathyld for her translation services.
To the Duchess, for being the better half of Team 888.
To Beefranck, for being the binding polymer.
And to my Mum, for being.

ABOUT THE JUROR

Jamie Chalmers, aka Mr. X Stitch, is one of the most recognized male embroiderers. Since 2008, he has been running the Mr. X Stitch website, which has become the hub of the contemporary embroidery movement, and is the co-host of Stitching n Junk, the world's greatest stitching podcast. He is an exhibited artist, having had his work shown in the US and Europe, and has curated contemporary embroidery exhibitions in the UK.

MOTHERBOARD_5
Created by Alicia Ross
2008 | 36 x 51 inches (91.4 x 129.5 cm)
Cotton; cross-stitched
Photo by artist (next page)

176